Spiritual
Power Points

Spiritual
Power Points

A Guide to Hidden Oases
Along the Spiritual Path

by Robert Krajenke

ARE
PRESS

**ASSOCIATION FOR
RESEARCH AND
ENLIGHTENMENT**

A.R.E. Press • Virginia Beach • Virginia

A.R.E. Press
Sixty-Eighth & Atlantic Avenue
P.O. Box 656
Virginia Beach, VA 23451-0656

Library of Congress Cataloging-in-Publication Data
Krajenke, Robert W., 1939-
Spiritual power points : a guide to hidden oases along the
spiritual path / by Robert Krajenke.
p.   cm.
Includes bibliographical references.
ISBN 0-87604-376-7 (trade paper)
1. Spiritual life. 2. Association for Research and Enlightenment. I. Title
BP605.A77K72   1997
299'.93-dc21   97-1685

Cover design by Christine Morgan

Dedicated to the unseen power which sustains us all

Contents

Acknowledgments

I would like to acknowledge that without the constant encouragement and support of a long stream of friends that stretches through the years this book could not have been written. A special note of appreciation goes out to Shirley Phillips and John Kendrick for their love and concern which showed up one evening as a synchronistic and undeniable sign to keep on with this book. Others who deserve special note are Tim and Sherri Decatur, Louis Reeves, Joan Holmes, Kent Draper, Haver Cole, Linda Beatty, the many friends at Detroit Unity Temple and the Virginia Beach Fellowship, Cindy Sol and Gerri McGhee of *PhenomeNEWS*, the editorial staff at A.R.E., and to my wife Lynne whose unique contribution to the unfolding of my soul has brought untold blessings in the most unexpected ways.

Preface

If we were to work backwards starting with the creeds, dogmas, rituals, and traditions which have grown up from inspired and rationalistic interpretations of the Bible, back to when the Bible itself was first put in print, back further to when it was written down, and then back even further to the original experiences of those who received the visions and actually created the texts, we would discover that large portions of the book, perhaps most of the book itself, were written in and about altered states of consciousness coming out of a relationship with a living, creative force.

And when we arrived at the beginning, we would also see the end—the practice of what true religion is: a personal relationship with a transcendent, radiant, loving, intelligent energy.

One night a man named Don, who ate too much, who drank too much, whose life was in a state of chaos and confusion, dreamed that Edgar Cayce had written the music to the words of the Bible and the music was the most beautiful music anyone could ever hope to hear. But when he asked where he could go to hear this music, no one could tell him. Nobody had actually heard the music, not in a very long time. All anyone could tell him was that those who had heard it long, long ago said it was the most beautiful music they had ever heard.

Then the dream scene changed. Depressed and dejected, the dreamer was back in his apartment. There in the corner of the room was an old traveling trunk, something he had never noticed before. Curious, he went to the trunk and opened the lid. There on the top of the many things that had been stored away was *Edgar Cayce's Music to the Words of the Bible.* The missing manuscript! It was his! He had had it all the time!

And with that flash of recognition, an indescribably beautiful chord of music flooded the dream and he awoke.

When I asked Don what the dream meant to him, he replied without hesitation: "If I can coordinate the Edgar Cayce readings with the words of the Bible, I will hear the music of the spheres."

When members of Edgar Cayce's prayer group asked the sleeping Cayce where they could find music for the Ninety-first Psalm, Cayce encouraged them with a challenging response: "Write it yourself," he said. "Many of you are capable."

The Cayce readings, especially when conjoined with

the Bible, constantly point us to the incredible dimensions of our soul—the creative potential within us that is so exceedingly grand and vast that we stand before it in disbelief. Where do we find in our culture such a vision of humankind and a hidden sketch of every individual's own sleeping prophet, sleeping artist, sleeping healer, lover, and alchemist?

When Don shared his dream I felt the impact of it as if it had been my own. It resonated deeply with my own experience with Edgar Cayce and the words of the Bible.

The Bible is founded on a living, spiritual dynamic that for many of us has been simply lost and forgotten, obscured by dogmas, sectarianism, and all the "sins" committed in the name of righteousness and religion. His dream was a perfect metaphor, a parable for giving voice to something deeply felt, and curiously beyond words.

A few years later in Holland, I was invited to teach at Davidhuis, a beautiful spiritual center in Rotterdam dedicated to the Edgar Cayce material. This was my first day of my first visit overseas, and Gidi Croes, one of the founders of the center, took it upon herself to welcome me. In the meditation room, we began to share our biographies as we got acquainted.

She grew up in a nonreligious family. As a child, she knew little about Judaism, but at school, she was ostracized and persecuted by her schoolmates for being a Jew. When war broke out and the Nazis invaded Holland, her family was forced into hiding in the same manner as Ann Frank and her family. Again, she had to suffer for being a Jew, without any understanding of what it meant to be a Jew.

After the war, she remained angry and bitter about her heritage. All it had brought her was persecution and no benefits. As the years passed, her bitterness and anger continued. The resentment poisoned many areas of her life, and it brought her eventually to a decision. Since she could never escape being a Jew, she might as well learn what it was all about. And as she began to explore her heritage and connect with her spiritual roots, a profound healing and peace began to ease her soul. As the healing continued, she began to explore other spiritual paths and traditions, including the Christ-centered teachings of the Edgar Cayce readings.

As Gidi's story unfolded, I was enveloped in an experience of parallel realities. Here was Gidi in front of me, telling her story, and through her aliveness, centeredness, and strength, I felt in touch with her soul. At the same time, I had a profound sense of the Old Testament traditions being watched over by "guardians of the archetypes." That is, I had a sense of the printed Bible, as we have it, as an extension into matter of a complete system of spiritual forces and energies which is guarded, watched over, and protected by a special hierarchy of spiritual beings. They maintain the energy and insure that the system remains an open channel to the earth.

It took years before Gidi was ready to turn to her roots, but when she did, the flow of life and light channeled through a system of Old Testament images, rituals, stories, and traditions revived her soul and connected her to living, transcendental spiritual essence. And when she was strengthened and nourished, her soul could expand outward even further, ever more universal in keeping with the energies of this age, and still remain rooted in her own soul-chosen cultural roots.

When I encountered the Cayce readings, I was soul-starved, too. I was not meaningfully connected to any spiritual tradition except that of a writer in search of a vision and a voice in an era of beatniks, hippies, and flower children. My search eventually brought me to my own dark hole, and I tumbled in. And in between fits of trying to dig myself out and digging myself in deeper, I heard for the first time "the music" Edgar Cayce had written to the words of the Bible, and what a symphony it was! I was spellbound as great teachers—Al Turner, Eula Allen, Hugh Lynn Cayce, Mae St. Clair, Herbert Puryear, and many others told about and interpreted the Edgar Cayce readings' story of creation, the lives of Jesus, the dynamics of the soul, dimensions of consciousness, the laws of cause and effect, dreams, meditation, and a host of other topics that were infinitely compelling, filling my dark hole with an array of stepping-stones for me to assemble for my own way up and out. My own spiritual heritage, Christianity, came suddenly and magnificently alive, like an explosive burst of fire leaping from a bed of dying coals!

For the very first time I felt something powerful connected to "religion" that wasn't archaic and oppressive. The Bible was no longer the completely obsolete and irrelevant book I had thought it was. Now it possessed a powerful, transforming spiritual energy that seemed to go right down into the depths of my soul, a healing power that suddenly made sense of what twelve years of nuns, priests, and teaching brothers had tried hard to deliver.

It has been over thirty years since the seed idea for this book burst open in the light of Edgar Cayce's Bible study recommendations. In the process of "giving form to the energy," the book has taken on an entirely different shape from the one I envisioned. To be truthful, it has taken on the form that I most resisted giving it.

Now that the challenge of writing it is over, the challenge of living it grows greater. As I sit here and write these final words, I wonder who will read it. How many will find it? Who is it meant for? Is there music in it for anyone else to hear? Or, in some peculiar way, was it just for me?

The book is complete, and I release it. This must be something like Moses' mother felt when she set her infant wonder child adrift in his little ark on the currents of the Nile.

Go river, flow, take this child;
Surely you know who is waiting and where to go.

Introduction
"Build It and He Will Come"

Field of Dreams, one of my favorite movies of the late 1980s, begins with a young man walking through an Iowa cornfield and hearing a voice with a mysterious message.

"Build it and he will come."

The man doesn't know what to build, or who will come, or why these enigmatic words are being spoken to him. Soon, he understands that he is to build a baseball field in a cornfield—a diamond virtually in the middle of nowhere. To make space for the diamond, he plows under acres of ripening corn, the family's cash crop, and to the chagrin and ridicule of relatives, friends, and neighbors, he proceeds to carry out the irrational promptings and mysterious guidance of the voice and builds his field of dreams. As he follows the voice, challenges arise and miracles unfold, but when the baseball diamond is built, his life and those of many others are changed forever.

The diamond is an ancient mystical symbol for the soul. On one level, *Field of Dreams* is a classic tale of the hero's journey. It begins with a call to action and a mythic task to perform. Dangers are confronted and fears must be overcome. Supernatural forces come to the aid of the hero who experiences redemption and transformation by carrying out his destined assignment.

The Bible is also about builders who follow the irrational voice of the Spirit. The children of the restless rebel Cain, the first murderer, are the builders of civilizations and the fathers of all the arts and sciences. While Cain's progeny are establishing the nations of the world, a child of Seth, Adam and Eve's other surviving son, hears a voice. The message is as unlikely and eccentric as being told to build a baseball diamond in an Iowa cornfield.

Noah is told to build an ark.

Build it and He will come.

For, that which leads to the Christ is the mind. And the mind's unfoldment may be that indicated from Abraham to the Christ. 281-63

Perhaps the real meaning and purpose of the Bible has more to do with building arks and diamonds than with creating churches or religious movements.

Ancient wisdom refers to the purified spirit as the "diamond body." The essence of a diamond is clarity, perfection; it is eternal, indestructible, and highly valued.

Baseball is played on a diamond. Noah's ark has diamond qualities as well. When Noah hears a voice, the storms are a long way off. He trusts the voice. His inner sensing mechanism is intact. He has time to build. When the deluge comes, he has a spiritually designed craft of solid internal structures capable of riding out great storms. As a central piece in an imperishable myth, Noah's ark is stamped from the same mold as the diamond.

Clarity of vision, stability of purpose, and spiritual perfection are among the qualities a "peculiar" and eccentric people who are "called" by the irrational voice of the Spirit must build as they experience the journey from "Abraham to Christ."

For a moment, imagine yourself in Noah's ark. Close your eyes. Can you imagine the solidness of the timbers of the ark? Can you look around and see the perfectly fitted, solid joints and feel the snugness and solidity of the ark. Marvel at the well thought-out design. Now hear the pelting rain, the lightning crashes, the mountainous surging waves—and at the same time, know you are safe. Know you are secure, well provisioned, protected.

Today, we are all living in times of great change, turmoil, and emotional upheaval. The storms are already here. The waves are already crashing. If you haven't built an ark, it's time to come aboard one that is already built. Just as Jesus said, "I have prepared a place for you." The symbolism in a baseball game is as remarkable as the Scriptures. The dimensions of the diamond and the relationship to its parts are as ritually precise as those given to Noah. A batter rises up from a place beneath the earth, a dugout, enacting the archetype of rebirth. From an assortment of bats, he tests and selects the one that feels the most appropriate for his task. Like the shepherd's staff, the bat is a symbol of his authority and power. It is the club of Hercules, the rod of Moses. It is life-force, life energy, and with it he is expected to do great things.

Bat in hand, he steps into the batter's box—a four square space representing time and space. The eternal soul is now encased in the four elements.

Standing on a mound inscribed by a circle, the symbol of timeless perfection, the pitcher faces the batter. In his glove, he has a small white orb, a hologram of unity and wholeness.

In life, we are all players, bat in hand, ready to face what life throws at us. Our heroic task is to connect with that sphere of wholeness flung from the holy hill in the center of the great circle of creation. When you connect, you get to advance. If you strike out, there is a whole cycle of waiting, but another opportunity will present itself. Your challenge, once you connect, is not only to get on base but to make it back home again!

In times past, people looked for gurus, masters, elevated beings to tell them how the universe fits together, how life works. But in this age, people want to figure it out for themselves. They want to connect with their wholeness and move toward Home.

When the protagonist in *Field of Dreams* hears the voice, he has no room in his current life where healing can take place. His life is predictable and secure, and he feels stuck in its meaninglessness.

His "field of dreams" emerges from his response to the tasks and challenges given to him by the mysterious voice that captures his energy and attention. In a remarkable way that is fraught with challenges, he touches all the bases—and with the help of his team— he creates a "new heaven and a new earth."

This book was inspired by a system of biblical cues recommended by the great American mystic, Edgar Cayce. Based on some of the most profound insights and intuitions of the Western spiritual tradition, this unique system of biblical "power points" has the potential to unlock the hidden power of the deeper mind and open the seeker to the beauty and treasures of the Higher Self. The power points go beyond metaphysical interpretations of Scripture to reveal a system of accessing spiritual insights and power while providing ways to make them practical and applicable in your life.

While the power points in the Cayce recommendations include Old and New Testament verses, this book focuses primarily on the Old Testament recommendations. The Old Testament is the foundation on which the New Testament is built. The Old Testament verses, as they become internalized and translated into the mental, emotional, and biological processes of the body create a stable structure through which the Christ Energies can manifest and express.

The system contained within the power points will help you to identify and connect with the three spiritual birthrights of the soul, and reveal a four-step process to reclaim that state of wholeness and sufficiency symbolized by the Garden of Eden. The power points of the Old Testament will help you discover your personal destiny principle in the Exodus story and reinforce and support the awareness of where the Source of your power, light, and creativity can be found. You will be instructed in the power and responsibility of your choices and use the Psalms favored in the Cayce readings to enhance your creativity, spirituality, prosperity, and endurance. In addition, four key concepts from the Cayce readings and specially designed guided experiences will give you tools to maximize the energy of each power point and make the energy more accessible in your daily life.

This book is designed for individuals who want more control over their minds and bodies.

It is dedicated to people who are seeking to mitigate or transform feelings of loneliness, depression, and powerlessness and who are seeking self-renewal and transformation.

If you are seeking insights and techniques for deepening spiritual power and intuition, this book is for you.

If you are a spiritual seeker who desires to build and internalize a pattern of universal truths into your soul structure for your next life, this book is your builder's manual. Here is a blueprint for an ark to carry you through the turbulent times while you build your "field of dreams"—a place within where the angels follow the love of their heart and play the games that enchant them.

In this age when so much ancient wisdom is being re-revealed, each of us has the opportunity to discover, uncover, and explore the power points of the soul. They are encoded in our bodies and imprinted upon our minds. They are the same laws, principles, and cosmic relationships that alerted Noah to build his ark and thousands of others to build their field of dreams. The laws are seen in the patterns of the archetypes illuminated through myth, science, art, religion, philosophy. All we need is the heart for the adventure and the discontent that stirs the soul.

The Bible as a Resource

For every illness, for every emotion, for every circumstance and affliction in life, for every dream, for every goal and hope, there is a something in the Bible that speaks to that condition—to heal the hurt, fortify the faith, clarify what is cloudy, and expand what is dimly perceived.

Edgar Cayce's spiritual practice was to read the Bible from cover to cover every year of his life and meditate daily upon its message to him. His readings are replete with biblical quotations, allusions, exhortations, commentaries, discourses, admonitions, prayers, affirmations,

7

and paraphrasing and synthesizing of biblical truths for every circumstance, disease, and human condition that inquiring minds could present to him.

Yet, with all that wealth and variety, his in-trance Bible study recommendations appear to be very selective and "task specific." In effect, a repetitive core of Bible verses are consistently recommended. The core of verse and chapter is fluid, seemingly adapted to the unique needs of the individual for whom the reading was given, yet in almost all these readings, many of the same verses are always present.

In actuality only a handful of people asked for and received Bible study recommendations from Edgar Cayce. In some cases, recommendations were spontaneously given. Mr. [1173] was one of the few who asked specifically which portions of the Bible it would be best for him to study. His reading described him as a very spiritually advanced soul, and his question to the sleeping Cayce was concerned with how he could best serve his fellow human beings. The Bible study recommendations given to Mr. [1173] contain almost all the power points of the core group.

> Q. What passages especially should he read in the Bible?
> A. The admonition of Moses [Deuteronomy 30], the creation of man in the first three chapters, the admonition of Joshua [Joshua 24:15], the 1st Psalm, the 2nd and 4th Psalm, the 22nd, 23rd and 24th Psalm, the 91st Psalm, the 12th of Romans, the 14th, 15th, 16th, 17th of John, 13th of 2nd Corinthians [1 Cor. 13?], and the Book of Revelation. 1173-8

During the course of this reading, Mr. Cayce had what he described as the "most marvelous experience" of his life. After finishing the reading, Cayce woke up. He was excited, awed, and thrilled. For the first time in all his psychic work, he had a direct experience of the Master while giving a reading.

Jesus had spoken to him. He had said, *"Be not afraid, It is I, for we have much work for [this one, (1173)] to do."*

We can only imagine what that encounter signified for Cayce. Typically, when Cayce journeyed for the information, he experienced himself going up a spiral from darkness to light. In the lower realms, the entities were gross and distorted. As he rose higher, the darkness gradually turned ever brighter and the beings he encountered more evolved. Eventually, he reached a Hall of Records where a bearded figure would give him the information being sought. Now, for the first time after giving thousands of readings,* Cayce had a direct experience with the Christ. It is hard to overestimate the importance of this experience. For Cayce, Jesus represented the highest and most trustworthy source of information, and the Bible study recommendations flow out of this contact. In light of this experience, the appearance of the Christ provides an imprimatur for the power points recommended in this study.

In one reading the emphasis is on lessons from the Old Testament:

Begin with the study of this in self and remember as though it were: this is the Divine speaking as to the self. Read it in Exodus 19:5. Then study and analyze the admonitions which are given by Moses, the lawgiver, when he was ready to depart, in the 30th

---

*Edgar Cayce reported that from 1910 until 1922, when the readings began to be documented, he had given as many or more readings than were later recorded.

of Deuteronomy. Then as that in the 91st Psalm, then the 23rd Psalm and 24th Psalm. These are as admonitions, not as that which would separate you from the social life but rather bringing into your personality and individuality the Divine which will attract you to, and be attracted to, that which will bring the greater harmonies in thy life. 5241-1

In the following, using an Old Testament foundation, the Cayce source promises the development of something "new."

... we would begin again to study—this time the Book. Begin with Exodus 19:5. Then read again and know thoroughly the 20th chapter of Exodus ... the 30th of Deuteronomy, and apply it in the terms of the 23rd Psalm. Thus ye will make thyself new.
                                                                  3428-1

Here the Old Testament pattern is integrated with New Testament recommendations:

Do study Scripture. Do analyze it. Begin with definite portions, as: Exodus 19:5. Then study thoroughly the whole of Exodus 20, then Deuteronomy 30 ... then the first ten verses of the first chapter of John. And then the 14th, 15th, 16th, 17th of John. And then the 13th of I Corinthians ... to become a little more patient, a little more sincere ... a little more of brotherly love to those who are high-minded ... 2969-2

And in this, almost the whole table of contents appears for what will be the core of this handbook:

Read, in the beginning, the third verse of the first chapter of Genesis and read thine own fate, thine own ability. For, whomsoever will may have the light within.

Then read again in Exodus 19:5, and who will be a peculiar people? They who keep the law of the Lord. What is the law? Thou shalt love the Lord, thy God, with all thine heart, thy mind and thy body, and thy neighbor as thyself.

Then read again Deuteronomy 30th, the whole chapter, as it were, to thee.

Then Psalms 24, 23, 91. For each bears a message to thee.

Then again in St. John 14, 15, 16, 17. Find when ye are on the pattern and when ye wander afield.

Then in the 12th of Romans and the 7th of Hebrews, ye will find thine own answer.

Not that these are tenets beyond that included in the love of God, the love of neighbor; rather as His last commandment: "I give unto you, love one another." 5308-1

I have often wondered why the Edgar Cayce source had such a preference for this cluster of Scripture. Edgar Cayce was such a finely tuned spiritual instrument as he lay in trance, and the documentation shows he was one of the most gifted clairvoyants of the twentieth century. During a reading, his superconscious mind was attuned to the subconscious mind of the person receiving the aid—and out of this attunement came a consistent but fluid core of Bible verses for meditation and study that addressed conditions ranging from loneliness and low self-esteem to a dedicated seeker's desire to better serve humanity.

"Be not afraid, It is I—for we have much work to do."

As we near the end of this century, there is much work for all of us to do. It might be the work of physical, mental, or emotional healing. It might be the work of parenting or of marital relationships, or of prosperity, stewardship, and service. It will always be work that is individual and unique to our peculiar life circumstances and our own response to the mysterious call of the "voice" of the soul.

The universal work is learning to love, to serve one another in a sacred manner, and to prepare a way for the Christ influence, the Christ spirit, to come again to rule and reign in the hearts of men and women everywhere.

And we are given all the help and support we need, if we just open our hearts and turn within.

SMALL DOSES, LARGE MEASURES

A heavy or exhaustive program of Bible study was never recommended in Cayce's psychic counseling. Rather the approach was one of small doses, large measures.

An example:

> Read only about five to ten verses each day. Then apply that given in those verses for a day! Then read five to ten more—apply that. You will find a regeneration. For, remember—thy body is the temple; there He has promised to meet thee. 2067-6

> . . . not too much at once—a verse or two verses—then meditate upon same as being an experience of self; not someone else but of self . . .
> 1317-1

Any verse in the Bible, any small grouping of words—

or even a single word—is, as the source affirms, "alive with the spiritual force of an all-wise, all-loving Father." (1231-1) Almost anything between the covers of the Holy Bible, including the cumbersome genealogies and the monotonous repetition of laws in Leviticus, can stimulate a spiritual experience. Even "the ordinances have their place in the awakening . . . of the inner being of a soul." (1173-8)

If words and images serve as memory keys, or power points, for releasing the energy which is encoded in the messages of the Scripture, then any word, phrase, grouping of verse and chapters contains a type of holographic power to link the receiver of the message to its Source.

Once the connection is made, a link is established that can be expanded by the seeker's mental focus and spiritual desire.

READ THE VERSES AS A DIRECT MESSAGE SPOKEN TO YOU

One of the most pointed recommendations in the Edgar Cayce Bible study readings is its insistence that the power and meaning of the scriptural message exists in the present, in the eternal Now, and not in the past, as tradition or creed.

For example:

> . . . in thy reading of the Scriptures . . . Read them not as history, read them not as axioms or as dogmas, but as of thine own being. 1173-8

> Use those texts or chapters as indicated as if the writer, as if the Father was speaking direct to the *entity*, to *self!* Read them with that understanding, that interpretation! 1231-1

Know they are not to someone else but to thee! . . .
For as He has given thee, "If it were not so I would
have told you." And this means *you!* 1299-1

The Edgar Cayce readings describe prayer as "talking
to God," and meditation as "listening for the answer."
Prayer and meditation are both keys to a direct and personal relationship with the Creative Force we call God.
So, it is not surprising that "listening"—meditation—is
an important aspect for enhancing our relationship to
the Scriptures. This is an important consideration. Too
often we defer to tradition or to perceived religious or
spiritual authority figures and discount our own intellectual and intuitive insights. Claiming your own internal wisdom or insight as your message "spoken directly
to you" is empowering and challenging—and a necessary step for building arks and diamonds.

MEDITATE UPON THE MESSAGE

. . . meditating on those commands, those promises, those warnings. They are the words of life; and
life, here, means that continuation of a consciousness, and the study of the relationships of self to the
Creative Forces or God. 1664-2

And during such a period make this the time not
for conversation but rather meditating upon the
possibilities, the probabilities, upon the Infinite as
it relates to and interrelates with constructive forces
within the minds of individuals. 949-5

As Moses gave of old, it isn't who will descend
from heaven to bring you a message, nor who
would come from over the seas, but Lo, ye find Him

within thine own heart, within thine own consciousness! if ye will *meditate,* open thy heart, thy
mind! Let thy body and mind be channels that *ye*
may *do* the things ye ask God to do for you! Thus ye
come to know Him. 281-41

As truth seekers, when we experience the rush of excitement of newfound spiritual truth, we go on a gallop-
ing high. Everything we read or hear is full of energy and
exhilarating mental quickening. Ideas and insights explode like firecrackers going off—pop! pop! pop! And we
rush like a child in a candy store, wanting to put everything colorful, shiny, and sweet in our mouths. We can
get addicted to the taste and never stop to wonder why
these ideas or verses have the impact they do.

The Edgar Cayce readings encourage us to be still and
wonder . . . and ponder. And meditate.

Meditation provides the opportunity to clarify the
message and to more directly experience our Genesis
birthrights—the light of God, the image of God, and the
power and presence of God. Meditation requires periods of withdrawal from the busyness of our lives and a
quieting and focusing of our mental and emotional activities.

COGNITIVE MEDITATION

In the Cayce source teachings, two forms of meditation are recommended. The first form is the classical
Western form of meditation. This is practiced through
reflection, introspection, by mulling something over in
order to explore and exhaust all the possibilities of the
most appropriate meaning for our understanding, purposes, or need.

For example, one individual was given this recommendation. Perhaps it suits your style as well:

> In the searching, then, begin with reading each day just a few verses of the 14th, 15th, 16th and 17th of St. John. First read in the 14th, "In my father's house are many mansions."
>
> Dwell on that, not for an hour or a minute but for a day—as ye go about your work.
>
> Who is your father? Whom does He mean, in speaking to thee? And what does He mean by mansions? and that there are many mansions in His house? What house? 3578-1

What is a father—physically, mentally, spiritually? Is he a protector, provider, teacher, guide? Someone older than ourselves? A potent, generative source?

What are your associations with a mansion? Is it just a big house, or does it imply more: power, influence, abundance, provisions.

And what does it mean that your Father—a potent, generative, creative force—has created one for you?

This form of meditation can take you to the dictionary to look up precise meanings, root meanings, and definition of terms. It can send you to original texts to "research" as much as possible—comparative studies, commentaries, interpretations, etc. Or cause you to delve into comparative religion, mythology—or into your own childhood memories and personal associations.

Perhaps we read someone else's interpretation, and it sounds good, or maybe another's interpretation doesn't quite fit for us. Or we need to break down old traditional interpretations to find a living essence in it for us, for today. Sometimes, we are drawn to a verse. It calls to us, and we don't know why. That's when we need to stop and look. To inquire and ask. We need to take it into our own closet and work it through to uncover the unique message it has for us. The subconscious mind will reflect back information and experiences from earlier periods in our lives, some of it good and some of it not so good. Much of it we may have outgrown or need to reinterpret or connect with again at a more adult level.

This cognitive, introspective style of meditation requires reflection and thought to complete and form ideals based on the meaning of the passages; then reword and rephrase the scriptural statements in terms of one's own understanding. Keep asking questions, keep turning up answers and new associations—until you reach your own inspired conception. Allow the meanings to continue to unfold and grow in your heart!

DEEP MEDITATION

The second form of meditation recommended is not a mental exercise but an emptying of self to facilitate a closer attunement with Creative Force. Deep meditation is the emptying of ourselves of all that would hinder the raising of the Creative Forces through the spiritual centers of the body. It is the attunment of our mental and physical bodies to their spiritual source or to the soul-mind. Deep relaxation and an emptying of self allows the creative energies to rise through the system, bringing an experience of our relationship and connection with divine energy.

The Cayce source defined meditation in this manner:

It is not musing, not daydreaming; but as ye find your bodies made up of the physical, mental and spiritual, it is the attuning of the mental body and the physical body to its spiritual source. 281-41

When a woman asked the entranced Cayce how she could gain more control over the power of her mind, the source responded:

> By more and more turning within. This would apply to material as well as mental and spiritual aids: Use a Radio-Active Appliance for *attuning* the body. And during the use of same, whether used daily or at set periods . . . use that period as a period of *deep* meditation; gradually raising, through the system, opening the centers of the body for better understanding.
>
> Then the activity of the bodily forces as attuned to concentration will make for not only a better feeling, physically, but an adaptability of the spiritual *developments* of the body *to* the material surroundings. Resentments and slurs will be more easily . . . forgotten forces, and the more positive aspect of Creative Energies flowing through the system become apparent. 1473-1

Do the work, practice the presence, and you are well on your way to "standing like a star" in the age of Peace.

OTHER MEDITATIONS

Other "meditative" approaches can also be utilized to deepen your experience with these Scriptures. These would include active imagination, mandalas, guided imagery, spontaneous or inspirational writing, poetry, creative art, dance, or music.

Enlist your dreams as another form of meditation. Being prayerful and focusing the mind on a Bible verse and repeating it to yourself as you go to sleep may bring you a revealing dream experience.

Creative writing, dance, and song allow you to amplify the feelings of your original insight or messages and to concretize your experience by putting it into a form.

YOUR TRUTH MUST BE LIVED

To complete the process of moving insight, messages, and attunements into the dynamics of change and transformation, your truth must be applied. No real change or learning takes place until it is tested in the area of relationships and ideals.

Read the Book, if you would get educated. If you would be refined, live it! If you would be beautiful, practice it in thy daily life! 3647-1

Read it to be wise. Study it to understand. *Live* it to know that the Christ walks through same with thee. 262-60

Until we can experience the truths in a personal way that are presented to us through the Bible, we have no real basis to evaluate or understand their merit and significance to our lives. By applying the "message" we receive in the silence of meditation, we make the principles and energies a part of our selves. Receiving and amplifying the message through meditation is only a preparation. The learning begins when we start to apply what has been given. Until the experience has been tested, assimilated, and digested, there is no lasting gain.

YOU WILL GET RESULTS

The wisdom in the Cayce readings stresses that knowledge of truth is not enough. To be fully understood, truth must be applied. To get the results promised in the Scriptures, you must put it into practice. It is guaranteed.

Characteristically, after recommending selected Bible passages for meditation and reflection, an array of "promises" was made in each reading, each promise fulfilling the deepest longings of various individuals. It will be the same for you, no matter in what incarnation you encounter them:

This kept as a rule, as one of the "musts" will save the entity many a disappointment in its dealings with men. 1664-2

. . . to become a little more patient, a little more sincere . . . a little more of brotherly love to those who are high-minded . . . 2969-2

And ye will find *peace*, and an awakening—beautiful! 1473-1

Thus ye will make thyself new. 3428-1

For in the study of these ye will find that ye draw unto that force from which the writers of same gained their strength, their patience. 1173-8

And ye will find that the attitude towards individuals, towards conditions, will have a much greater meaning; bringing into the experience harmony and an activity worthwhile. 1231-1

These are as admonitions, not as that which would separate you from the social life but rather bringing into your personality and individuality the

Divine which will attract you to, and be attracted to, that which will bring the greater harmonies in thy life. 5241-1

REVIEW:

The Edgar Cayce readings advocate a threefold process of using the Bible for spiritual growth and development.

1. Read the verses as a personal message to you. Small doses for large measures.
2. Meditate upon the message.
3. Test the message by applying it in your life.

Remember to keep balanced and expect results.

A SUGGESTED EXERCISE:

Spend a few minutes reflecting on your needs.

Write a list of areas in your life where you need healing, help, or change.

Write what you hope to gain from your Cayce Bible study experiment. What is your expectation?

What do you feel you need or want to have happen in your life to make the expectation a manifestation? Are you willing to do whatever it takes to see it through?

Write down what's troubling you. Then spend time considering how your life would be different if you no longer were troubled by these things.

Find a quiet place to meditate and allow your inner self to guide you as you focus on the questions above.

Now store these notes someplace and forget about them for a while. After six months or a year, as you progress with the power points experiment, bring them out and read them again. Have your expectations been met—or exceeded? How are you different now than you were then? Which of the power points has the most energy for you?

BUILDING ARKS, BUILDING DIAMONDS

One of Edgar Cayce's own readings suggested his name should be changed from Edgar to John. As an aid to carrying out his soul's purpose, the vibration carried by the name John would assist Cayce better than the name Edgar, because—the reading stated—as a forerunner, or herald of the Christ in this age, he was in a position relatively similar to that of John the Baptist in his time.

In addition, Edgar Cayce is regarded by many as the "father" of the holistic health movement and an important influence in the development of parapsychology as a science in America. As a psychic diagnostician and spiritual counselor, he is widely regarded and acknowledged for the efficacy of his treatments and the accuracy of his diagnosis. In addition, Edgar Cayce was a lifelong Bible student and Sunday school teacher. These remarkable abilities and roles make his Bible study recommendations all the more compelling. The verses represent some of the deepest and most profound mystical intuitions and metaphysical insights into the nature of our relationship with God, or the Creative Forces, or Universal Consciousness we call God. This is not to say that these verses are more exalted or sublime than other passages of the Bible, rather they gain their significance by being the part of a pattern, or system, of verses most frequently offered for study by one of the great spiritual giants of the twentieth century.

Each of the verses has its own potential "message" for you, and its power is even more enhanced by the special synergy that comes with the unique coupling of the passages with one another, which is another special characteristic of the Cayce recommendations.

Perhaps there is an alchemy in this system of biblical power points—an organic unity that, in effect, reflects a refined and distilled essence of the entire Scripture.

If you are curious, the only way to know is to test them in your own life.

THE RECOMMENDATIONS

Now it is time to turn to the heart of the matter—that wonderful and powerful fluid core of chapter and verse drawn from the rich and awesome wisdom of the Edgar Cayce source.

SPIRITUAL POWER POINTS
based upon recommendations
in the Edgar Cayce readings

OLD TESTAMENT:	Key Ideas
Genesis 1-3	Spiritual Birthrights
Exodus 19:5	Destiny and Purpose
Deuteronomy 30	Choice and Source
Exodus 20	Foundation Principles

PSALMS:	
Psalm 1	Wisdom Teaching
Psalm 8	Angels and Our Place in Creation
Psalm 23	Universal Prayer
Psalm 24	Economic Healing and Meditation Experience

Psalm 91   The Lord's Prayer of
                                  Protection
Psalm 150   The Ultimate Conclusion

In the New Testament, the Cayce source repeatedly suggested that people study the life of Jesus and people's experiences of Him, John 14-17, Romans 12, Hebrews 7 and 11, and the Book of Revelation. The New Testament recommendations will be the subject of a future book.

A SUGGESTION:

In the next section, all the verses are reprinted from the New Revised Standard Version of the Bible. Read them in the recommended manner of "small doses," taking time to meditate upon the meanings.

Record your insights, revelations, thoughts, and feelings in a journal—your "new testament."

Be aware of which verses carry energy for you and which are neutral. Notice the ones which are positive, uplifting, and pull upward on the soul. And observe the verses which provoke negative reactions. Be curious to know why.

Meditate upon those which evoke the strongest feelings, both negative and positive, and record your feelings.

Pay attention to the themes and reoccuring images you find interwoven throughout the verses. How relevant are they for you in your spiritual journey today?

If you are studying this material in a group, focus your attention, discuss only a verse or two at a time, and decide on ways to "test and apply" your interpretations in your daily life. Share the results together.

Recall the words of Jesus in Edgar Cayce's "most marvelous exerience." *Be not afraid, it is I. We have much work for this one to do.* That message was given to one spiritual seeker. Could that be a message for you as well?

Exploring Creation

Q. What passages especially should he read in the Bible?
A. . . . the creation of man in the first three chapters . . .
1173-8

In the beginning, God created the heaven and the earth.
And the earth was without form, and void; and darkness was
upon the face of the deep. Genesis 1:1-2

THE WISDOM OF THE EDGAR CAYCE READINGS

The earth and the universe, as related to man, came into
being through the *mind—mind—*of the Maker . . . 900-227
For in the beginning God moved and mind, knowledge,
came into being—and the earth and the fullness thereof
became the result . . . 5000-1

Mind is the Builder.
Consciousness is the initiator of Creation.
What God thinks, is.
What I think, I am.
What my thoughts dwell upon, I become.
As I think God's thoughts, I bring forth Light.

You are, indeed, at the beginning of a "new heaven and a new earth." This simply means, by reading this book and through your willingness to explore the principles in the readings and the Scripture, you are at the beginning of initiating a change in your concepts of and relationship to Spirit and matter and to the energy we call God and to the creation we call humankind.

According to the Edgar Cayce readings, our first existence was as a consciousness in the Mind of God. Our first awareness was that we were spiritual beings in a spiritual world—a perfect place to begin. We are an indivisible part of a dynamic universe, and we are constantly changing—even the cells of our bodies change with every breath we take, with every thought we think.

In the Gospel of John, Jesus prays, "*O Father, glorify thou me with thine own self with the glory which I had with thee before the world was.*" (John 17:5) He also asks that His disciples may know that same glory that He knew before the world existed. The glory relates to a state of oneness, a state of awareness—a memory of that place in the Mind of God where we all began—the perfect place to begin.

Through the discoveries of quantum physics, we know that the smallest particle in the universe is not a piece of matter called the atom but a quantum measurement of light called a photon. By some mysterious process, energy becomes matter, Light becomes flesh. The mystery is unsolvable and profound. No matter how much we may change, lose, or forget—we can never be less than this Light, the building block of matter, the source of Creation. Light is the source of every atom of our body, every neuron in our brain. It is the substance that is the glue of the universe and was fully possessed by Jesus when He said, "I am the Light."

As we align with that Light, we will, by design and destiny, begin to remember that we are expressions of the Divine. When our consciousness is attuned to and activated by Divine Ideas, our spoken words are infused with spiritually creative energy. We feel the form of the archetypes—the perfect patterns—and joyously co-create with Divine Intelligence. That is our birthright. And the earth and its fullness will be the result.

Thus Cayce's admonition, "Mind is the Builder."

Or the injunction of Paul, "Be ye transformed by the renewal of your mind."

Or, "Put on the mind that was in Christ."

EXPERIENCE THE BEGINNING

Richard Heinberg in *Memories and Visions of a Lost Paradise* indicates that there are thousands of creation myths told among the world's peoples, yet out of the multitude of myths concerning the "Beginning," there is only one story and four basic themes.

The one story is that in the beginning humankind experienced unity with the Divine and with nature until something occurred to disrupt the relationship, causing separation, pain, fear, terror, and aloneness. Since then, we have been trying to return to the Beginning.

Heinberg identifies the four themes as:

CREATION OUT OF NOTHING: A solitary Creator-God brings forth Heaven and Earth by the potency of His thoughts or the creative power of His words.

THE COSMIC EGG MYTH: The Universe unfolds from the dynamic interaction of primordial masculine and feminine energies, or the yin and the yang.

EARTH DIVER STORIES: A representative from the upper world of Spirit plunges into the unformed chaos and dredges up pieces of mud to form the entire world.

EMERGENCE MYTHS: The original people emerge

from various realms of the underworld into the bright daylight of the physical world.

While all these stories attempt to portray humankind's cosmic origins, these stories are also taking place within us with every new thought, every new beginning. One of the great sacred universal truths is that we are one with the Divine, and at the same time, we have forgotten our relationship and separated from it. All of humanity, either consciously or unconsciously, is trying to mend that relationship and restore oneness. We are creating and re-creating the same timeless story in our own unique and individual ways.

Indeed, we are composed of the interplay and dynamic of opposing energies of the Cosmic Egg myth. The opposite polarities of negative and positive energies—of male and female, passive and active, conscious and unconscious polarities—create flowing currents of life force which knit the diverse elements of our many aspects into an organized and dynamic creative energy that we call the psyche or soul. These energies are knit and woven into our every thought and action, and become reflected in our bodies.

In every meditation, in every experience of introspection and self-analysis, we are reliving the Earth Diver story—inviting a Higher Consciousness into our awareness that frequently stirs up the contents of the unconscious within, causing us to re-form and reshape our mental and emotional worlds. The same is true in the emergence myths. Like seeds planted deep in the earth, powerful energies arise from out of the unconscious to burst forth and bloom in the (symbolic) light of consciousness.

And we are constantly creating "something out of nothing."

The Edgar Cayce teachings follow the "creation out of nothing" myth of Genesis. Creation begins in the Mind of the Creator, first as a Divine Idea on the inner planes of reality, before manifesting—through sound—in the outer world of form.

As the readings indicate, everything in the Bible is capable of being experienced.

Let's explore.

In the Beginning, the spirit of God is moving.

The spirit of God is moving—where? Across the waters, over the face of the deep.

Consider in this moment that your body is almost entirely composed of water. On the physical plane, it is a creation of fluids, of waters. Your blood, your cell tissue, your lymph system, your circulatory system, every organ, every nerve fiber, every cell ending is filled with fluids—water—circulating, moving, flowing through your arteries, your veins.

With every breath you draw, with every inhalation, the spirit of God *is* moving across the waters.

And the earth is without form and void,

and darkness is upon the face of the deep.

What could be deeper than what is not known? It far surpasses what we know.

Einstein suggested that we use less than 10% of our brain's capacities—perhaps, as little as 1% to 3%, some believe. Yet, our brains function at incredible speed—one hundred billion brain cells functioning in perfect synchronization, generating fields of energy—brain waves! Each brain cell is a miniature computer with incredible processing abilities, transmitting chemical messages instantaneously to trillions of cells through the whole body in a continual cascade of neurotransmitters.

What could be deeper than your own ability, your own potential, the unmasking of your own unknowing of how vast, how deep the power, the presence, the spirit of God is within you.

And the earth is without form and void,
and the spirit of God is moving across the void.

Can you imagine a void—a vast space filled with emptiness? All matter is mostly empty space. At the quantum level, your physical body is composed of atoms, and atoms are mostly empty space. But the emptiness of the atom, like the emptiness of intergalactic space is an emptiness filled with an energy scientists call "virtual energy"—the raw energy of unmanifested potential. Virtual energy is the source of infinite possibilities and the first cause of all creation. It is the substance of all space, shaped by Mind, the omnipresent Divine Intelligence.

The emptiness is all your potential held in suspension, until called forth in consciousness to become a new possibility!

Your body is a universe of atoms—billions of atoms. And inside the atom, the particles that make up the atom—the protons, neutrons, and electrons—are as proportionally distant and vast from each other as the distance that separates the earth from the sun! Can you imagine your body as a universe of particles dancing in a cosmic void packed with incredible energy? The energy in this body of emptiness is the spirit of God filling all space.

As you breathe, even while you are relaxed, even while you are still, breathing slowly, deeply, energy is moving and incredible processes are occurring throughout your body. The creative intelligence within you creates a brand new skin every thirty days. Every five minutes, the surface cells of your stomach renew themselves. Every four days, the intelligence and the energy moving through you creates a whole new stomach lining. In six weeks, all the cells in your liver are replaced.

In your body all the conditions for a " new heaven and a new earth" are present. What is your concept of "heaven," of "earth"? New understandings of spiritual consciousness and matter are forming in your mind and are being registered through your body's responses.

And God said, Let there be Light—and there was a new impulse of intelligence, of enlightenment, drawn from the totality of all possibilities that exists in the emptiness of a billion times a billion atoms in your body. And there is Light, a spark of insight flashing in the chaos of our own unknowing, calling us to the mystery of who and what we are. A new beginning!

All begins in consciousness.

Mind is the Builder, and the physical is the result.

Divine Ideas! Spiritual Patterns! Mind in harmony with the Word, and you the result!

What could be more spectacular!

CREATION: A GUIDED EXPERIENCE

Let us explore!

Find a quiet place where you will not be interrupted or disturbed.

Get in a comfortable position, and speak the words of Genesis 1. Speak them loudly and clearly, knowing somehow they relate, not to a distant past, but to you right now.

In the beginning God created the heaven and the earth.
And the earth was without form, and void;
and darkness was upon the face of the deep.

Speak them out loud, exploring the different sounds in the words.

What is the sound of Spirit moving across the face of the waters? Can you find that tone in your body? Which sound or tone carries the most energy for you?

Allow your imagination to create the scene painted by your words.

What is the feeling of a formless void?

What is your image of chaos existing throughout creation?

Imagine now, the Spirit, the Divine Presence—the activity of God—moving into chaos, filling a great void. What happens next? Have you ever had an experience where a condition of chaos and confusion was suddenly brought into order and peace through the appearance or presence of a special person, object, or event? What did that feel like?

Now, in this relaxed state, become aware of your breath. Everything begins with your breath. As you inhale, focus your attention on the feeling evoked by the image of "the spirit of God, the spirit of creative activity, moving across the waters." Be aware at the same time, that your body is almost all water. Breathe in a slow, steady cycle of inhales and exhales. Creation is taking place. Something divine, something sacred is emerging out of the formless void of your unconscious and coming into awareness.

As you breathe, allow your feelings to merge with the biblical image. Your breath is the spirit of God moving over the deep parts of yourself. Every breath initiates and adds to the creation you are becoming. With every breath, you bring forth light.

With every breath, the molecules in the air that you breathe in instantaneously attach themselves to the hemoglobin of your red blood cells—and there is light. The dark blue-black of oxygen-starved hemoglobin, now rich with oxygen, turns bright red.

In the brain, billions of neurons, each as complex as a small computer, fire an electrical signal that triggers the release of complex neurochemicals and links it with thousands of other neurons. Ten thousand neurons synchronize and, for one hundred milliseconds, flicker all at once like a strand of Christmas lights, followed by the illuminations of ten thousand more.

Continue to breathe in and out in a slow, steady rhythm. With each thought, each image in your mind, millions of synapses in your brain burst, explode, with fire. Millions of cells light up like stars in the void, and instantaneously these lights bond with the molecules, sending chemical messages throughout your body, and millions, billions, trillions of cells in perfect synchronization respond instantly to each message.

The spirit of God is moving on the face of the waters, and creation is taking place.

What is the source of your ideas, your visions, your hopes for the future? Where do they come from? From what source do your feelings arise? Where are they held?

What is it you want your life to be?

How will you shape your environment in order to feel the depth inside you and know the spirit of God moving across the waters.

A MEDITATION FOR YOUR ATOMIC ENERGY

In Genesis Adam is created from the "dust" of the earth. The "dust body" is, of course, a reference to the soul—the divine image—and its container, the physical body. Dust, the smallest and most abundant particle of matter visible to the naked eye, is a metaphor for the atom. In those days they didn't have a word for "atom"—but *Adam* is pretty close. The ancients recognized that the physical body was composed of billions of tiny particles held together by an invisible energy and that this energy was related to the Divine Source. They used the metaphor of dust to implant this idea in the subconscious mind of the uninitiated. It was something that was easily understood but that also pointed to other realities.

Through the image of the void, the ancients expressed another reality. From a quantum point of view, almost everything about us is empty. The atom, the building block of matter, is virtually 99.99% empty space. The electrons, the protons, and neutrons that whizz around each other and form the atom are so minute that the spaces separating them are proportionally as large and vast as the spaces between the stars in intergalactic space. Since we as humans are made up of atoms, the same is true of us. Only a fraction of what we are is composed of particles of matter. The rest is consciousness, energy, potential—emptiness.

But if we are mostly void, the emptiness is an interesting one. Unless you can see it filled with angels, spiritual guides, and radiant cities of light, the intergalactic void among the stars appears cold, bleak, and lifeless. Yet, as seen by a physicist, the void of inner and outer space is packed with "virtual energy"—an awesome, creative force waiting to coalesce into atoms, into molecules, into ideas, forms, stars, planets. As Deepak Chopra says, citing a five-thousand-year-old perception from ancient Ayurvedic philosophy, we exist in a Field of Intelligence filling all space, containing the totality of all possibilities. Isn't it exciting to consider that the emptiness we feel inside is the raw energy of unmanifested potential? No wonder we can transform sadness into elation or depression into action. The emptiness is all your potential held in suspension, until called forth in consciousness to become a new possibility!

Water has always been used as a symbol for Spirit. At the level of physical manifestation, our bodies, with all their marvelous complexity, intricacy, and miraculous systems and functions, are virtually all water. At the spiritual level, the atomic body—the soul—is composed almost entirely of sea stuff, too—the pure energy of the cosmic ocean.

POWER POINT MEDITATION: DUST BODY

Find a quiet place. Take a few relaxing breaths, and relax. Clear your mind, and with the next breath, become aware of your body. Sense its weight and be aware of its volume, the shape, and the relationships it forms in the space around it.

Now move your attention from your body to the chair, or whatever is supporting your body now. Is it soft or solid? Round or rectangular? Smooth or textured? Consider how easy it is to accept the existence of matter for what it appears to be: solid, real, dense, observable. Now understand, as is known by science and known even longer through intuition and ancient wisdom, that everything you are and everything you touch and taste and feel is a dancing field of subatomic particles expressing infinite possibilities in a field of intelligence.

Take enough time to feel it. Just a few moments will do, and then release the image. See yourself now standing on a hilltop on a clear summer night. You are looking up into space, at a great field of stars and feeling the energy of the universe flowing through you, feeling awed by the mystery and yet one with the whole. Take a few moments now to immerse yourself in the feelings, and when you are ready, release the image, and on your next breath, go into your body. Follow your breath into your lungs. Be aware of your heart beating, of blood and oxygen and nutrients traveling through your veins and arteries. Be aware of your brain sending signals to your legs, your muscles, your internal organs, to your fingers and your toes.

Now with your next breath, focus on any part of your body that comes into your awareness. And when you have that part of your body fixed in your mind's eye, pluck out just one atom from the millions and billions of atoms that surround it and bring it before your mind's eye. In your imagination now, focus on that atom. Can you imagine something smaller? Split the atom, and split it again, and you have something smaller yet. Keep splitting each particle until there is nothing left to separate— until there is only the energy from which the first particle sprang.

Now, wipe the image from your mind, and bring back the atom. With your imagination and trusting the amazing ability and processing power of your unconscious mind, move your awareness into the center of this single atom. Notice the particles whizzing and orbiting around the center, the nucleus. Allow your imagination to take you to the center of the atom. As you stand in the center of the atom, looking out from the heart of the nucleus at the particles whirling around you, you understand that the distance separating you from them is the same as the distance that separates you from the sun and stars, and you feel in this tremendous emptiness the energy of the atom. Allow the energy of the atom to saturate your consciousness, allow it to flow through you until you merge with the virtual energy in this ocean of emptiness.

Now gently guide the atom back to the place in your body where it belongs. See it instantly merge with the field of other atoms, and as you pull back you are aware of the energy of millions and billions of atoms in your body. Breathe in again—feeling the energy and the light, feeling the intelligence that fills the vastness of the void—and feel all the unlimited possibilities that the potential you contains. Allow now the incredible lightness of your Being to transform the illusion of materiality into Light. Enjoy your atoms. Enjoy your molecules, enjoy your cells—and all those empty spaces! When you are ready, open your eyes and slowly come back to your ordinary consciousness, feeling totally renewed, refreshed, energized.

Reflect for a few moments on your experience or, if you choose, write your impressions in your journal.

CONTINUE CREATING: AN EXERCISE

In the Cayce readings, God and Creative Energy are synonymous and interchangeable terms. The more freely and naturally we express our creativity, the more of our God-Nature we can experience and reclaim.

To encourage this process, you are invited to explore further with the following exercise:

You will need art supplies and a large sheet of paper or your journal and a pen.

Spread out your paper or open your journal. Without thinking ahead or allowing fear and self-consciousness to inhibit you, focus on your breath again and the images and feelings of your breath experience with meditation on Genesis 1. Begin to describe the sensation of the creation. Write it from any point of view you like—as an angel, as the wind, or the surface of the deep. As chaos or darkness. Or from the center of the atom. Allow the Spirit to move you.

Be creative and write without reflecting on its literary value—but rather use the writing (or artwork) to create an experience with the archetype, with the images of Creation—and with your own deeper reserves of creativity and feeling.

Three Birthrights of
the Spiritual Creation

At its most energetic and esoteric level, the Bible is a system of encoded power points that are designed to light up the unconscious. Every verse in Scripture is a potential power point. The power points are concealed in symbols, images, affirmations, and allegories. Each has its own holographic power and all are part of a system that leads to the discovery of the deeper mind and the beauties of the Higher Self. Even the ordinances and the genealogies, one reading states, have their place in the awakening of a soul.

In *Fingerprints of the Gods,* Graham Hancock adds his

name to the growing list of scholars and scientists whose research supports the Cayce information concerning the existence of lost and forgotten prehistoric civilizations with cultures far superior to ours. Their ancient myths, like their grand monuments, Hancock states, were designed to carry information into the future—information which we are now in the process of discovering and decoding. We are a species with amnesia, he writes, and it is time to recover our memory.

THE FIRST BIRTHRIGHT

MIND MADE AWARE: THE BIRTHRIGHT OF LIGHT

And God said, let there be light.
And there was light. Genesis 1:3

THE WISDOM OF THE EDGAR CAYCE READINGS

He, that Christ Consciousness, is that first spoken of in the beginning when God said, "Let there be light, and there was light." 2879-1 The *Spirit* moved—or soul moved—and there was Light (Mind). The Light became the light of men—Mind made aware of conscious existence in spiritual aspects or relationships as one to another. 1947-3

Then, it is necessary for the reliance upon Him, who is the truth and the light, who from the beginning was that expressed in, "And God said, let there be light; and there was light." . . . For without Him, without light, was not anything made that was made, this applied, this fact conceived, this truth lived in the daily life will put away fear and doubt of every nature. 3188-1 And there is little or nothing that may separate a soul from being perfect in body or mind, even in the earth, save self. For, the spirit is willing and all that is necessary for this correction has been given in the earth, in "Let there be light."3320-1

Do study creation, man's relationship to God. 3491-1 Read, in the beginning, the third verse of the first chapter of Genesis and read thine own fate, thine own ability. For, whomsoever will may have the light within. 5308-1 Find that Light in self. It isn't the light of the noonday sun, nor the moon, but rather of the Son of man. 3491-1

In Genesis 1 we find three power points that form an indestructible core of our spiritual identity. These are our birthrights of Light, of Divine Self-Identity, and of Mastery and Control. They cannot be lost, sold, or given away. Our only choice is whether we, as divine creations, will claim them.

In the Gospel of St. Thomas, an ancient Gnostic text, the disciples ask Jesus, *"Tell us how our end will be."* The Master answers: *"Have you then discovered the beginning so that you can ask about the end?"* And he completes his teaching, adding: *"Where the beginning is, there also shall be the end."*

Spiritually this is a powerful teaching that gives us much to ponder. Our beginning and our end are one. Did we begin in chaos or did we come into existence through the Light? If we feel lost, uncertain, unfocused, or undermined with a vague sense that we are not everything we are meant to be, we need to recognize that this is a sign of our amnesia. We have, at the deepest level, forgotten who we are; we have lost connection to the life-affirming Source Image of our own creation.

As the Edgar Cayce readings indicate, Creation first begins in the Mind of God. As a symbolic description of a spiritual process, Genesis 1 describes a perfect beginning. It is the beginning of coming to consciousness—of restoring our memory of who we are, where we came from—and where we are headed. This "beginning" is available to us through the practice and experience of meditation.

God says, *Let there be Light!*—and there is Light. In a state of darkness (unknowing) and chaos (confusion), the first perception and experience of divine truth appears and begins to rearrange the chaos to manifest as a spiritual pattern expressing a divine idea.

The Light of Perception provides the momentum and the energy that initiates the first of many cycles of alternating energies of light and darkness until the completed work of the Divine Creation is made manifest through us. As each cycle of light expands through continued meditation and the practice of spiritual growth, we are able to see more and more of the Divine operating in and through us. These cycles of development continue as the new perceptions are expanded, lost, regained, experienced, and developed and integrated through altering cycles of understanding and expansion, of confusion and chaos, of growth and mastery, of stagnation and overcoming until finally we reach the understanding of who we are —"divine images"—and from this realization we receive the power (be fruitful and multiply and have dominion) to fearlessly be who we really are!

And who is that?

Respond with your feelings in your journal.

Affirmation:
I affirm my birthright of Light.
I affirm my birthright of Divine Self-Awareness.
I affirm my birthright of Mastery and Control.
I awake to the Divinity of that I AM

and claim and affirm all the birthrights
and heritage inherent in God's Plan for me.

THE SECOND BIRTHRIGHT

THE BIRTHRIGHT OF DIVINE SELF-AWARENESS

So God created man in his own Image,
In the image of God created he him;
male and female created he them.
                                    Genesis 1:27

THE WISDOM OF THE EDGAR CAYCE READINGS

And remember, man—the soul of man, the body of man, the mind of man—is nearer to limitlessness than anything in creation. 281-55 For the image in which man was created is spiritual, as He thy Maker is spiritual. 1257-1 For while the body changes, for it—too—must be purified, the *soul* remains ever as one. For it is in the image of the Creator and has its birthright in Him. 1243-1

The biblical power points are keys to our deepest memories, and the most profound sequence of these power points is located, appropriately, in the beginning, in the very first chapter of Genesis. Sandwiched between "Let there be Light" and that awesome, misunderstood, and misapplied affirmation of our inherent capacity for self-mastery, "Be fruitful and multiply and subdue the earth," is, perhaps, the most treasured of the mystical affirmations of our Western spiritual tradition, the assertion of our Divine Identity.

I often wonder how many people take this verse seriously. Here is the cure for a poor self-image and a power boost for your self-esteem. But first it requires a well-formed concept of what God is. What is it exactly that we are an image of? There is a blueprint within us, but do we know how to read it? Ask most people if they believe that we are made in the image of our Creator, and almost everyone will respond with a yes. But ask them to describe the "image," and the responses are usually vague, general, and lacking in power.

One of the most beautiful and awesome passages in the Bible takes place in Job 38. You know the story. Job was a fine, upright citizen whom God permitted Satan to tempt. Job is beset by endless challenges and suffering. Through all his trials, Job affirms his innocence and, despite the unmerited sufferings, never loses faith in God or blames Yahweh for his afflictions. After enduring endless advice from his "comforters" with all their metaphysical insights and moral platitudes about his fall from grace, Job finally has a direct experience with Yahweh. Appropriately, Yahweh challenges Job about his ability to remember the Creation.

"Where were you when I laid the foundations of the earth?" Yahweh sings to the stricken Job. "Tell me if you can. Surely you know!"

The fateful question seems like the impossible test given to the heroes of the great myths and fairy tales who must solve a dilemma or lift a curse before a princess can be freed or a treasure gained or a kingdom healed. To the ancient Gnostics, Yahweh's actions seemed like those of a petty tyrant, not a sublime divinity. While His taunting may have sounded like bombast and sarcasm to these Gnostics, Yahweh's questions also imply a capacity to bring to remembrance events and measures of cosmic dimensions. Manly Palmer Hall in *Old Testament*

Wisdom writes that the Book of Job carries echoes of initiation rituals of the ancient mystery schools. When Job is asked, "Where were you . . . when the morning stars sang together and the Sons of God shouted for joy?" an answer was expected. These questions were designed to awaken, rather than shame. Job is a parable of the soul's journey through materiality. His afflictions, like ours, may be due to "forgetting."

Which brings us back to our question. Are we confident about our beginnings? In the Gospel of John (14:26), Jesus promises to send a Comforter who, when we are ready to receive it, will teach us all things and restore all things to our memory.

Do we have the faintest memory of our deepest roots—our true ground of being?

How far back can an individual's memory travel? Through how many lifetimes?

When you say, I AM, who or what are you affirming that you are?

Eula Allen, author of the Creation Trilogy and one of the most gifted interpreters of the concepts in the readings on the spiritual creation, always began her Bible class with an observation from her teacher.

"Mr. Cayce always said that the key to understanding the whole Bible was found in The Revelation." And then, with a smile and glint in her eye that left us fledgling Bible students with the impression we may have begun our study with the wrong book, she added the punch line, "But he always said, you can't understand Revelation until you understand Genesis."

You have to know where you came from in order to know where you going.

A purpose of the Edgar Cayce life readings was to stimulate awareness of previous life experience, so the constructive influences of that incarnation could be brought more fully into consciousness to aid the individual in its development and growth in the present.

In several life readings, including Edgar Cayce's, the Edgar Cayce source sought to stimulate memories and awareness of the soul's connection to this primal, joyous, harmonious spiritual experience of the Beginning. For example:

> . . . in the beginning, when the first of the elements were given, and the forces set in motion that brought about the sphere . . . called [the] earth . . . and when the morning stars sang together, and the whispering winds brought the news of the coming of man's indwelling, of the spirit of the Creator, became the living soul. This entity came into being with this multitude. 294-8

> . . . when the earth's forces were called into existence, and the Sons of God came together, and the sounding of the coming of the Man was given. This entity was there. 234-1

At the end of his ordeal, Job sees God face to face and joyously proclaims, "I have heard of you by the hearing of the mouth, but now my eyes see you." At this instant Job is truly enlightened. His enlightenment brings a shame to be overcome and a yearning for the transcendent to be fulfilled as Job recognizes both his old egotism and limitations—"I abhor myself and repent in dust and ashes"—but now he has also seen the splendor of the Divine Source, in whose Image he is made, and lived.

Not only is all that he had lost restored to him, but his blessings and prosperity are multiplied. He is more powerful, prosperous, and fulfilled than before.

Eric Butterworth, a bestselling author and Unity truth

teacher, states that the best kept secret of the ages is that you are the activity of God expressing itself as you. The "divine image" verse is a great truth to be taken seriously, he states. Anchor the thought in your consciousness that an All-Wise, All-Loving, Intelligent, Compassionate Creative Force is expressing Itself as you. Affirm this repeatedly, Butterworth states, and your poor self-image will begin to fade away and in its place will come a healthy awareness of your rightful place in the Divine Flow.

Divine self-awareness is a spiritual birthright. It cannot be lost, sold, or given away. Our only choice is whether we, as a divine creation, will claim it. The Great Intelligence which created the Universe hardwired the Divine Image into our DNA so we could never forget who we are, no matter in what form or body or dimension we may choose to appear.

If you can't remember who you are, the first thing to do is to clear up the confusion about who you think you are and what you think you are.

You are not your body.

You are not the roles and identities you have assumed.

Nor are you your feelings and emotions.

You are the energy which creates them.

It is sometimes very challenging to accept that somehow, at the deepest, truest, most essential part of ourselves, a template of the divine image exists within, expressing itself as us. As bearers of the God-Image, we have a vast, unlived, unlimited, untapped potential within—abilities and capabilities which, at our present level of consciousness and evolution, even the most advanced of our species are incapable of imagining.

In the mind of God, we can never be less than that perfect Image in which the Perfect Mind first visualized us. In our own eyes, we are whatever we see. Our perceptions determine our reality.

MEDITATION EXPERIENCE

In a quiet place, at a time when you won't be interrupted or disturbed for ten or fifteen minutes, take a few deep breaths to clear your mind, relax, and repeat the following sequence of these affirmations.

Focus on the feeling behind the words, and let the words/feelings carry you into your true I AM:

> *In the Beginning, I began.*
> *I began when Light came forth.*
> *I AM that Light.*
> *The Image of God expresses itself as Me.*
> *I AM the Power to Be.*

As you repeat the words, let go of all other "I AM" identifications until you experience the "divine image." Stay with the feelings for a few moments, and as you return to your normal consciousness, give thanks that your memory is being restored, and act accordingly.

My Spirit wills that I become perfect
In body, mind, and soul in the earth.
As I encounter resistance
to the perfect working out of God's Plan for me,
I affirm my birthright of Light —
LET THERE BE LIGHT,
The Light that was in Jesus,
The Light that was in Mary when she conceived him.
This is the Light that allows me to see
I am an Image of God
expressing myself as I AM.

THIRD BIRTHRIGHT

THE BIRTHRIGHT OF DOMINION

And God blessed them, and God said unto them,
Be fruitful, and multiply, and replenish the earth, and sub-
due it:
and have dominion over the fish of the sea, and over the fowl
of the air, and over every living thing that moveth upon the
earth. Genesis 1:28

THE WISDOM OF THE EDGAR CAYCE READINGS

Remember oft that command given, "Be fruitful and
subdue the earth." *That* is man's heritage. The earth, in this
sense, means all forces from without. These forces, these
abilities, lie before thee. Be up and doing! 279-5 For the
powers within must be spiritualized. Not that the body
is not spiritual-minded, but there is the necessity to be
spiritual-minded and then [be] able to gain control
sufficiently over the power of mind in the body as to
cause the vibrations from the atomic structures to produce health-giving forces . . . For know, as was given
from the beginning, it is necessary to subdue the earth.
Man is made, physically, from every element within the
earth. So, unless there is a coordination of those elements
of the environs in which the animal-man operates, he is
out of attune—and some portions suffer. He must contain and command those elements. These are subduing,
using, controlling; not being controlled by but controlling,
those environs, and influences about same. 3455-1

If the soul be perfect in its purpose and ideal—whatever the state may be, it will call on the Lord. It will rely
on the Lord. It will use every measure to comply with His
will and purpose. His purpose was for man to subdue, to

conquer, to use, to apply the earth in its every use for man. 2828-5 For His promises throughout the ages have been, "*Subdue* the earth," subdue the earth that is within thine own self! 689-1 . . . as may be literally interpreted from the first chapters of Genesis, ye find that those that subdued—not that were ruled by, but subdued the understandings of that in the earth—were considered, or were in the position of the wise, or the sages, or the ones that were holy; in body and mind, in accord with purposes. 5749-7

As I align my mental and spiritual ideals with the purposes and nature of the Divine, I am more than a conqueror—I become one with my divine heritage. And that which I hold in consciousness is suffused with creative force and will become a reality.

The closer I move to the Source of all power, the more powerful I become.

The closer I move to the Source of all health, the healthier I become in body, mind, and spirit.

The closer I move to the Source of all peace, harmony, and clarity, the more peaceful, harmonious, and clear is the energy I manifest.

The power of God is greater than any of its manifestations. The Cause is superior to its effects. Peace, harmony, health, love, creative powers have their Source in Truth. All disease, all sorrow, limitation, and pain have their origin in error and confusion.

All error and confusion in our lives can be re-ordered and eliminated by focusing on the Source of Truth and Light.

I claim the Birthright of Dominion—of my godlike abilities and purposes—to overcome and transform any effect, any condition, any disorder in my life and in my affairs that is not in harmony with the Divine.

POWER POINT REFLECTION

As you affirm, *Let there be Light*, breathe in the awareness of a divine energy illuminating you. Feel it throughout your entire body. When the mind begins to wander or your body, through urges, ticks, and twitches, demands your attention, "subdue the earth" by bringing your attention back to the feeling and the image of a Light-filled you.

As you attune to the Light, you are claiming a spiritual birthright that is yours by design and destiny, and the deepest parts of your soul will come forward to assist you as you persist in the practice.

You are designed for mastery and dominion—not of others, but of self!

One Breath from Eden

"Every day is an opportunity to wake up in Eden."
Edgar Cayce, Tuesday Night Bible Class

Tradition tells us that in order to preserve the integrity of their spiritual wisdom and sacred teachings, the ancient rabbis hid their truth in strange and childlike stories. Their sacred stories contained symbolic codes and numeric keys that could lead the seeker to profound philosophical insights and mystical truth and could provide access to transformational energies. The biblical story of Adam and Eve is one of those stories. One of Edgar Cayce's sayings from his Bible class was "Every day is an opportunity to wake up in Eden." A careful reading of the story in Genesis 2 reveals four power points we can use to make his knowing our reality.

Cayce's wonderful little metaphor implies that we are asleep, forgetful of a potential condition or state of being that is ours to claim each day.

Eden is a place we have all experienced. Eden exists as a memory of wholeness, of a consciousness of supply and abundance, a place where all our needs are continuously and uninterruptedly met in a spirit of Love. On one level, Eden represents life in the womb and the innocence of childhood experiences. Some claim Eden is a racial memory, stored in the collective unconscious and preserved in the mythologies of the world, of an actual pristine, golden age when humanity was much closer to the world of Spirit. Eden is a dream state rooted in soul memory, a forgotten condition that can only be reclaimed by striving for a new and higher level of consciousness.

The ancient sages knew in future ages, the memory of the "Beginning" would grow dim and get lost. And in their wisdom they created imperishable roadmaps to guide us to that mystical place of self-renewal we are calling "Eden."

What keeps us from Eden consciousness? The incessant overtones of guilt, worry, resentment, and shame build barriers. Or, as Deepak Chopra states in *Perfect Health,* the rage, fear, fantasies, wishful thinking, and unfulfilled dreams that constitute our internal dialogue keep our minds and bodies too distracted and tense to perceive the landscapes that lie at deeper levels of the soul. We stay fixated on patterns of awareness and perception rooted in memories and feelings of the past. These fixations are the source of illness, depression, sadness, addictions. The darkness described in Genesis 1:1 covers the deep, resourceful part of the psyche where our wholeness is experienced. It remains hidden until the

Divine Within says, "Let there be Light"—and we begin to remember who we are, "Divine Images."

Genesis 2, in a remarkable way, offers a four-step system back to wholeness.

WAKING UP IN EDEN

THE FIRST PRINCIPLE: THE BREATH OF LIFE

And the Lord God formed man of the dust of the ground, and breathed into his nostrils the breath of life; and man became a living soul. Genesis 2:7

THE WISDOM OF THE EDGAR CAYCE READINGS

For, was not the physical being made from all else that grew? For, of the dust of the earth was the body-physical created. But the *Word*, the *Mind*, is the controlling factor of its shape, its activity, from the source, the spiritual— the spiritual entity. Thus there are within the abilities of each soul that ability to choose that as will keep the body, the mind, the portion of the spirit, attuned to holiness— or oneness with Him. 263-13

THE BREATH OF LIFE

Adam is the first to "wake up" in Eden and, thus, is the prototype for all of us who are asleep in Paradise. How does the process of "waking up" in Eden begin? The opportunity exists with your next breath.

God breathed into his nostrils and Adam became a living soul. Gen. 2:7.

To find yourself in Eden, you must first point your mind toward it. As the Yoga sutras of the Patanjali affirm, "Mind follows breath."

Have you ever taken a deep breath and counted to ten to calm your anger or take control over other emotions? Or taken in healthy draughts of fresh air to invigorate your body and oxygenate your cells? Or practiced the Edgar Cayce head-and-neck exercise or other forms of yogic breathing? Every breath we take is a healing breath. Every breath has the power to awaken deeper awareness and resources. Practice conscious breathing. Take a moment to close your eyes, relax, and repeat this seed thought to yourself, "I am a living soul." Be aware that each breath is the breath of life. As you breathe in the breath of life, focus your awareness on the affirmation, "I am a living soul." You've taken the first step to entering your Eden. Repeat the affirmation with each inhale for the next few minutes. Your breath provides you with the power and the ability to awaken to a consciousness of your spiritual nature. Continue, and you will get closer to Eden with every breath.

AFFIRMATION:

My breath gives me the ability to awaken to a consciousness of my spiritual nature, to the awareness "I am a living soul."

THE SECOND PRINCIPLE: CHOICE

And the Lord God commanded the man, saying,
"Of every tree of the garden thou mayest freely eat:
But of the tree of the knowledge of good and evil,
thou shalt not eat of it: for in the day that thou eatest thereof
thou shalt surely die. Genesis 2:16-17

THE WISDOM OF THE EDGAR CAYCE READINGS

Karma is met either in self or in Him. For, as has been given, "in the day ye eat thereof—or in the day ye entertain fear, the day ye entertain sin—the soul must die." Not in that moment, possibly not in that era, but if the soul continues in sin, that is karma, that is cause and effect. 2990-2 For, as given of old, each soul shall give an account of every idle word spoken. It shall pay every whit. And this is as self-evident as the statement, "In the day ye eat thereof ye shall surely die." It is as demonstrative as, "Be ye fruitful, multiply, *subdue* the earth." 3124-1 But God has not willed that any soul should perish; He has with every temptation prepared a way of escape. 2990-2 Thus there are within the abilities of each soul that ability to choose that as will keep the body, the mind, the portion of the spirit, attuned to holiness—or oneness with Him. 263-13

PATTERNS OF GROWTH, PATTERNS OF CHOICES

After Adam awoke, aware that he was a "living soul" expressing in a dust body, his next awareness was that he had to make choices. In Bible symbolism, trees represents "patterns of growth." In Eden, God grew *"every tree that is pleasant to the sight and good for food."*

As spiritual beings, we have the divinely bestowed privilege to delight in and cultivate "every tree"—every pattern of growth—a human body can express.

However, if we are to regain our Eden awareness, we must cultivate from the tree that is in the center of the Garden, the Tree of Life. We can create "choice patterns" that enhance the consciousness of Oneness, or we can continue experiencing duality by partaking of the knowledge of the opposites.

We are designed to sustain the consciousness of One. Through the gift of free will and a Creative Spirit, God encourages and permits us to explore and develop many "patterns of growth" and to taste the fruit of every outcome. Choose what you will, but if the pattern you create is not in alignment with divine purpose, with the universal laws of good, of growth—then the fruit of your activity may be bitter indeed.

If you want to experience the Light, you have to harmonize with the laws that produce light. If you want to be love, you have to harmonize with the laws that produce love. If you want to be prosperous, you have to harmonize your mind and spirit with the energies and principles that create prosperity.

Jesus said, "I come to give you life and life more abundant." We are divinely endowed with abilities to express and experience in infinite ways. We are also responsible for our choices. And our choices create our experiences.

The second power point in the Eden story is the awareness of our free will and our ability to make choices.

Choose "life" by engaging in activities that support a spiritual awareness of your relationship to the One Source, such as meditation, and you won't be far from Eden. But the ancient rabbis tell us there is more to do.

AFFIRMATION:

I am a living soul. My choices keep me attuned to the Life-giving spirit of God.

THIRD PRINCIPLE: NAMING

. . . and whatsoever Adam called every living creature, that was the name thereof. Genesis 2:19

NAMING THE NAMES

Even in Eden, amidst the plenty, Adam was incomplete. He was lonely. To heal that loneliness, Adam was given a task to do. All the creatures of the earth were brought before him to be given a name. But of all that he saw, none could he call by the name of "that which takes away my loneliness."

Like Adam, we all have a task to do with each incarnation. An incarnation is not a random happening. We must identify essences and establish relationships in ways that make us whole and complete. For most of our lives, we may be "naming the animals." And as busy and preoccupied as this may keep us, in the end we may still feel lonely and incomplete. This may have to do with the "names" we give to our experiences.

Naming is a way of identifying or defining relationships. When we give a name to something or someone, we identify a relationship to it. We identify an "essence." Adam had to name everything that passed before him. In a similar manner, we have to "name" everything that comes to our attention—every thought, every action, and every feeling. We name them as good, bad, pleasureful, undesirable, evil, blessed, happy, sad. This is our birthright as "images" of Divine, Creative Energy. If we choose to identify our difficult, painful, or uncomfortable experiences as "problems," then that's what we get. *Problems!* But if we name them "growth lessons" or "initiations" or "opportunities for soul development," we are claiming power over events and using them for our greater good. The real name is not the external tag or label we attach to some one or some thing. The "name" that determines and defines that nature of our relationship to the person, thing, or event springs from the emotional response (or reaction) that it raises in us. If you smile when your mother's sister visits and call her Auntie Sue, but in your heart you groan and grimace and refer to her in unkind terms, which name defines who she really is to you?

Naming, then extends to the name we give ourselves and others. As Carol Pearson so cogently observes, if we do not accurately and objectively name ourselves and our own stories, then we will be at the mercy of how others see us and will be defined and re-defined by a vagrant and off-the-wall voice in our head:

> Every time we name a reality in such a way that we diminish people or possibilities, we are, however inadvertently, acting out a bit of evil sorcery. We are naming people in a way that lessens their sense of possibilities, their self-esteem, their capacity to see hope for the future. One powerful way to transform your life is by changing the way you name your experience. The impulse to accuse ourselves is heavily ingrained in this culture. Instead of seeing yourself as sick, inept, or clumsy, or dwelling on the past or future mistakes, it is possible simply to trust yourself absolutely, and to know that you choose and

will choose everything that happens to you for your own growth and development. Doing so restores dignity and adventure to life and transforms even the most seemingly negative circumstances into opportunities for growth.*

By identifying the spiritual purpose or lesson contained in each experience life presents us, we gain dominion over negative forces by minimizing them and aligning ourselves with life-affirming creative values. By naming our realities from the point of view of the soul, we lay claim to a powerful tool for empowering ourselves and others.

If we can see "purposeful experiences" in everything that happens to us, that becomes the name of our Creation.

Continue to name your experiences "good," "leading to wholeness," and "empowering" and you are that much closer to feeling whole and complete.

In the Book of Revelation, a reference is made to a white stone with a new name written on it "which no man knoweth saving he that receiveth it." This name is given and revealed to "he who overcomes." (Rev. 2:17) This name is not written on any birth certificate or family tree. Before we can ever find this name, we must look within.

This takes us to the fourth and final power point of the Garden fable.

AFFIRMATION:

Whatever name I give to a person, thing, or condition, that is what it becomes.

---

*Carol S. Pearson, *Awakening the Heroes Within—Twelve Archetypes to Help Us Find Ourselves and Transform the World.* HarperSanFrancisco, 1991, p. 198.

THE FOURTH PRINCIPLE: I FIND
WHOLENESS BY TURNING WITHIN

*And the rib, which the Lord God had taken from man,
made he a woman, and brought her unto the man.*
                                            Genesis 2:22

THE WISDOM OF THE EDGAR CAYCE READINGS

Q. *Is the destiny of woman's body to return to the rib of
man, out of which it was created? If so, how; and what is meant
by "the rib"?*
A. With this ye touch upon delicate subjects, upon
which *much* might be said respecting the necessity of that
union of influences or forces that are divided in the earth
in sex, in which all must become what? As He gave in
answer to the question, "Whose wife will she be?"

In the heavenly kingdom ye are neither married nor
given in marriage; neither is there any such thing as sex;
ye become as *one*—in the union of that from which, *of*
which, ye have been the portion from the beginning! 262-
86 [For] how received woman her awareness? Through
the sleep of the man! Hence *intuition* is an attribute of that
made aware through the suppression of those forces from
that from which it sprang, yet endowed *with* all of those
abilities and forces of its Maker . . . 5754-2

THE FOURTH PRINCIPLE

It isn't until *the Lord God caused a deep sleep to fall
upon Adam* and the famous piece of bone is taken from
his side that Adam finally experiences wholeness and
completion. The rib, of course, is drawn from within
himself. And what was within him, which had been pre-

viously unknown, overlooked, and unnamed, becomes his companion and soul mate. An old alchemical principle states, "That which was the least prized, most despised now becomes the greatest treasure in my eyes." The rib is the undervalued, missing portion of ourselves that makes us complete. The little piece of rib, like the mustard seed, appears small and insignificant and easily overlooked—yet when taken from within Adam, when brought into consciousness and named "other self" and "beloved companion," becomes his greatest treasure.

NOTES ON ADAM AND EVE FROM A KABBALIST

Unlike English, which was developed to communicate very pragmatic and concrete realities, Hebrew has always been uniquely structured as a vehicle for identifying, expressing, and explaining sacred and subtle spiritual truths and identifying and articulating internal levels and degrees of consciousness.

Each letter of the Hebrew alphabet is a hieroglyph, and has an intrinsic numeric value, with the number representing a vibrational frequency or energy pattern that identifies a quality, aspect, or function of Spirit. Rather than a name composed of letters, a Hebrew word is a combination of "hieroglyphic" images and vibrational patterns. The combination of images and frequencies of each word suggests a variety of possible meanings and levels of interpretations to the intuitive researcher and spiritual seeker.

The name Adam in Hebrew is composed of three letters, Alef, Dalet, Mem. Master Kabbalist, Sam Bousky, renders the "hieroglyphics" as:

Alef Sacred Life force that is related to a Divine Source

Dalet A passageway that permits life force to enter into creative growth

Mem Divine formative substance. *

In the original Hebrew, the kabbalistic meaning of Adam does not indicate a male, but rather a generic term for humankind. Adam, as a designation for the physical body, identifies it as a "container" for the Spirit. According to Samuel Bousky, the mystical meaning of the Hebrew letters suggests that ADAM is a "container with a doorway that permits the entrance and processing of spiritual forces, or energies."

In other words, Adam is a name for our bodies, identifying both the endocrine system of the physical body and its corollary, the chakra systems of the subtle body.**

A Kabbalistic Exercise:

Meditate upon the three concepts suggested by the letters above. Try to visualize them as components of a single essence. On a sheet of paper, write out your understanding of the combined letters and you will have

---

*These and the following comments relating to the kabbalistic interpretation of Adam, Eve, and Eden are based on notes taken from lectures and conversations with Mr. Bousky.

**The Edgar Cayce readings indicate the endocrine system, or ductless glands, function as "doors" or points of contact between the electromagnetic energies of the physical body and spiritual energies of the soul.

reached your own interpretation of the inner meaning of the name *Adam*. Next, describe how your interpretation relates to yourself.

Eden is made up of three letters, Ayin, Dalet, and a final Nun.

Ayin   Activity, or flow, supportive of growth

Dalet   Doorway, entry

Final Nun   Purpose for attainment of spiritual growth.

The inner meaning of Eden embedded in the Hebrew letters suggests Eden represents a statement or a condition which permits the entry of activity for spiritual growth, such as a condition of inner harmony.

The inner meaning of the word wife or woman in the ancient Hebrew is expressed by the letters Alef, Shin, Heh.

Alef   Fire

Shin   Divine

Heh   Radiance.

Divine Radiant Fire represents our intuition, inner knowing, and creativity, the irrational and psychic dimensions in our totality. Thus Adam's soul mate Eve is the "divine, radiant fire" of his inner being. Bringing Eve from within him, as a part of him, into his consciousness represents a condition of inner balance or harmony with the creative forces, or "sacred fire" or "inner light."

In the external world of "containers," where conformity and predictability is valued highly, and where most identify with their bodies, the "divine fire" has often been "the least prized, most despised" of our possessions, because it is not predictable, easily controlled, or "reasonable." It is the subjugated "feminine" energy that is now reasserting itself throughout the planet in order to restore balance. Adam's wholeness is completed in a passive way, by becoming receptive, still—through "sleep"—dreams, meditation, reverie. As long as we are looking outside only, we can never feel whole and complete. Our true companion doesn't exist "out there." Our true "soul mate" is exactly that—our soul! We will discover the power of the rib by turning within and finding the treasure there that makes us complete. When we realize and experience this, we have truly arrived in "Eden." It is ours to discover today.

Breathe in and meditate upon it.

AFFIRMATION:

I contain that within me which makes me whole and complete.
My inner self is my true companion, my "soul mate."

A SUMMARY OF THE PRINCIPLES

By practicing the principles so wisely concealed in Genesis 2, we will discover our opportunity to "wake up" in Eden every day.

The Principle of Breath (Gen. 2:7)
The Principle of Choice (Gen. 2:17)
The Principle of Naming (Gen. 2:19)
The Principle of Companionship and Completeness
(Gen. 2:21-22)

Each principle, as it is applied, leads us to deeper levels of awareness.

"I AM A LIVING SOUL"

In the first chapter of Genesis, God says, *Let there be Light.*

In the second chapter of Genesis, God breathes into Adam and whispers, "Let there be *Life."* The Light becomes a living soul.

Genesis 1 is crowned with the creation of the Divine Image—*male and female created He them.* Genesis 2 finds its completion in a "divine image"—a perfect union of the male and female principles in an ideal setting supportive of spiritual awareness.

Adam, with his first breath, woke up in Paradise. With your next breath, you can too. God is an equal opportunity Creator, the same today as a million years ago. We need only to become still and focus on our breath. Every breath we draw is the breath of life. Every breath we take is an opportunity to wake up to the awareness that we are "a *living* soul."

EXERCISE: AWAKENING

Here is a simple exercise to begin your awakening.

Find a quiet place and simply focus on your breathing. Be aware of your inhalation and your exhalation. As you begin to relax, remain aware of your breathing cycle. It sustains you. It activates life-supporting processes in your body. It allows you to "wake up" to the reality that you are experiencing life through a marvelously designed body capable of processing spiritual energies.

As your mind settles around the awareness of the sacredness of your breath, repeat the affirmation, "I am a living soul," with each inhalation. As you reach the peak of the inhalation, take a quick short breath in, as if impressing the image on your subconscious mind, and hold your breath for a few seconds and exhale. Continue breathing, fully aware that this breath is the breath of life and impressing the image in your mind with the final rapid, short inhalation as you focus on the affirmation. Continue until you begin to feel an inner balance.

When you feel this inner balance, focus your attention on your power of choice. Make a conscious decision now to go even deeper into this experience. Make a choice to stay connected to the awareness that you are a Living Soul, and stay with that awareness for the next few breaths. Realize now that you are creating a "pattern of growth" toward oneness. You are becoming a Tree of Life.

As you continue with the experience, identify it with a name or names that carry you deeper into a more complete and whole experience with your "other self." Repeat the names silently or aloud.

When you are aware that the body is completely relaxed and the mind is alert and the names have taken you as far as you can go, cease with all techniques and efforts. Surrender control. No longer guide the experience. Allow the "divine radiant fire" of the inner self to reveal itself while you "sleep."

And when the experience feels complete, slowly return to your normal consciousness, and record your experience in your journal.

EXERCISE: SPIRIT INTO MATTER

Mind is the controlling factor of the body's shape.
262-13 (paraphrased)

Creation was a joyful event! In the beginning, "the morning stars sang together." (Job 38:7) In several life readings this reference to the morning stars is incorporated in descriptions of the spiritual preparations for the earliest appearances of man in the earth.

> . . . in the beginning, when all forces were given in the spiritual force, and the morning stars sang together in the glory of the coming of the Lord and the God to make the giving of man's influence and [the] developing in the world's forces [this entity was there]. 2497-1

> . . . when the forces of the universe came together, when there was upon the waters the sound of the coming together of the Sons of God, when the morning stars sang together, and over the face of the waters there was the voice of the glory of the coming of the plane for man's dwelling. In all of these we find some of this present entity's individuality, and in some, some personalities are brought through. 341-1

> . . . when the earth's forces were called into existence, and the Sons of God came together, and the sound of the coming of the Man was given. This entity was there. 234-1

> . . . the entity was in the beginning, when the sons of God came together to announce to matter a

way being opened for the souls of men, the souls of God's creation, to come again to the awareness of their error. 2156-2

THE MORNING STARS ARE SINGING

In the readings quoted above, several reasons are suggested why, in the very beginning, a pristine soul dwelling in a spiritual dimension might choose to take on a "dust body" and enter into the earth. We might consider these the "original choice," a positive complement to the doctrine of "original sin":

. . . to be an influence in the evolution of man's development
. . . to use the human body as a vehicle to make manifest heavenly—or spiritual—forces
. . . to help souls understand their errors—their separation—and demonstrate a means, or way, to correct it.

POWER POINT EXERCISE

In the realm of classic myth, the forces of Light and Dark, good and evil are always clearly drawn. There is always a good guy and a bad guy doing combat with each other, with the triumph of good, or natural law, as the ultimate victor.

As a great myth, the creation story in the Cayce readings recount that as the "Divine Images" entered into the earth, they separated into two streams of creation. Those who used their creative powers selfishly, for self-aggrandizement, are identified as the Sons of Belial. Those spiritual entities who chose to express their energies and gifts in harmony with divine law were identified as Sons of the Law of One.

Their chief impulse for coming into the earth was to find a way to reach the Sons of Belial and restore the fallen or lost consciousness of their Divine Source in them. However, as they became enmeshed in the earth forces, they followed the pattern of Adam in the Bible, and they fell into forgetfulness as well.* However, because they bear the imprint of their original choice for coming into the earth, they are continually seeking those experiences, even at an unconscious level, to rekindle the light that will direct them back to their spiritual purpose.

THE ORIGINAL CHOICE—
AN EXPERIMENT IN CREATION

If you are reading this book and others like it, you are most likely one of the souls who originally entered in the beginning with a high spiritual purpose. You have always carried a memory of this purpose with you. Do you remember your original choice and what it felt like, as a spiritual being, to make it? This power point exercise is designed to help you experience some of those energies. Be playful! Have fun! Remember, Creation was a joyful event.

Stand with your knees slightly bent, your feet apart lined up with your shoulders.

Take in a deep breath all the way down to your navel, and affirm to yourself, "*I am a spiritual being.*" Bring the feeling all the way through you.

Now, with your next breath, be aware that you are a

---

*For a more detailed and complete version of the Creation story, see *Edgar Cayce's Story of the Old Testament,* Volume 1.

conscious spiritual being and affirm, "*I am a spiritual being with a mind. I am spirit and mind indivisible.*"

Breathe in again and recognize your ability to make choices and affirm *I am a spiritual being of Mind and Light with the ability to make choices.* Breathe that awareness into your aura, into your energy field, and feel it all the way through your body. Feels good, doesn't it, knowing you are a radiant, spiritual being of imperishable Light and fantastic creative energies with the power of free will.

In this moment, just for now—feel all those feelings. When it feels the best you can make it feel as a creative spiritual being, take your hand and, as if plucking a handful of virtual energy from the air, take the handful of that invisible, atom-filled substance of the universe and imagine it is a part of God, a drop of divine mind indivisible from the ocean of Intelligence that fills all space. And take this energy, cup it in your hands, and begin to shape it into a ball, a ball of golden energy. Feel the shape of the ball as it grows bigger and bigger, brighter and brighter until you have the amount of energy that feels exactly right. And when it feels exactly right, place your hands on the top of your head. As you feel this golden energy at the top of your head, imagine that this golden light of illumination fills your awareness now and you, as a spiritual being, as a creative, spiritual-mental being, are now fully aware of the purpose for which you chose to come into the earth at this time.

Breathe in this golden energy all the way down to the tips of your toes, until this gold energy and the shape of your body are one.

Now take your hands from your head and allow the energy to come through your hands as you rub them together, creating another ball of golden energy. Roll the energy in your hands. Feel the shape of the ball as it grows bigger and bigger, brighter and brighter until it feels exactly right. When it feels exactly right, place your hands over your solar plexus and gently push this beautiful golden energy in your emotional center. What kind of energy level will you need to carry out your purpose in the earth? How much courage and strength and persistence? Now for a few moments, allow the amazing processing ability of your deeper mind to assimilate this golden energy and shape it according to your soul purpose and desire. Feel the energy of your spiritual purpose shaping your internal organs, the organs of digestion, assimilation, and elimination into the perfect body for the experiences, the lessons of this lifetime.

Now rub your hands together again and shape another golden ball. Place your hands just below the navel, or on your hips, and feel the energy flowing through your hands into your stomach, your hips, thighs, through your legs, your feet, over the arches, all the way down to the tips of your toes. As this energy flows down through your legs and toes, a tremendous confidence comes over you. You know that this Light has created all the support you'll ever require to take the stands you need to fulfill the purpose of your spiritual journey in the earth.

Now take your hands and pluck another piece of the virtual energy from the substance around you and, in a rapid, circular motion, rub your hands together until you have generated a ball of golden energy. Roll it with your hands until you feel it vibrating with possibilities and potential. And when the energy feels right—not too much so your body can't handle it and not too little so you won't have the energy to do what you want to do—take this golden ball of light and place it over your heart. Feel the energy flowing through your hands, flowing into your heart, spreading like a beautiful sunrise through your whole upper body. As the Light fills and flows

through your heart, again a deep and profound awareness comes with it, imprinting every atom and molecule
with the understanding that your heart, your whole upper body is able and capable of staying motivated and
confident at all times of fulfilling your purpose in this
lifetime. Now remove your hands from your chest, rub
them quickly together again, creating a supercharged
ball of light and press your hands to your chest once
more, totally and completely thrilled by the challenge of
giving love, of receiving love in the earth until you have
given and received the full measure of love required to
fulfill your purpose in this lifetime and to restore harmony in the universe.

And now, you are almost finished. There is one last
thing to do.

Once again, you rub your hands together, creating a
great golden ball of light. And when the amount of light
is just right—and only you can know what is the right
amount of Light for you—not so much that it is overwhelming and blinding, and not so little that you feel left
in the dark—take that ball of Light and press that energy
into your hands until you feel its energy flowing out
through your fingertips. And when you do, press very
lightly with your fingertips the center of your forehead
just above and between your two eyes. And as you do,
your mind and the light become one. You are very wise
now, wise enough to know that forgetting your spiritual
purpose is part of the experience you'll have in the earth,
and the way of awakening is what you will search for and
share with others. And as the energy floods your mind
and thoughts, you understand totally and completely
that you are intelligent enough, alert enough, curious
enough, and wise enough to seek and find your purpose,
even when clouds of dust shaken by the turmoil and
challenges of the earth body should cloud it over.

With your fingers still lightly touching your forehead just as the point called the third eye, say silently or aloud, "Let there be Light."

With your next breath, breathe in and affirm, "I am a living soul," and feel through the power of your words this golden light activating all the systems of the body so everything works according to the divine plan in a smooth, harmonious way.

Touch the top of your head, the crown chakra—and feel this center with its knowledge of divine ideas and spiritual patterns becoming imprinted and illuminated.

Place your hands on your neck and feel the golden illumination filling and imprinting the seat of the will around the throat area with knowledge of the divine plan and divine will.

The three higher centers of your spiritual body are glowing with Light.

The four lower centers are fully illuminated.

You are perfectly designed to do what you have come to the earth to do.

Now with your eyes still closed, take a few relaxing breaths, fully aware that you are a spiritual being, a living soul uniquely designed to fulfill a special purpose in the earth. Feel yourself "materialize" now as you become more and more aware of your physical body. Wiggle your toes. Stretch your arms. Open your eyes slowly. Take your time. Enjoy the experience.

And when you are ready, record your experience in your journal. Or share it with another.

Was it easy or difficult to imagine yourself as a spiritual being, as a consciousness only?

Do you agree a physical body is not a requirement for conscious existence?

What is your spiritual purpose for coming into the earth?

Encountering the Serpent

Evil Trickster or Teacher and Guide?

Now the serpent was more subtil
than any beast of the field
which the Lord God had made. Genesis 3:1

And the serpent said unto the woman,
Ye shall not surely die:
For God doth know that in the day ye eat thereof,
then your eyes shall be opened,
and ye shall be as gods . . . Genesis 3:4,5

. . . that first awareness of deviation from the divine law
is given in the form as of eating of the tree of knowledge.
Who, what influence, caused this—ye ask?
It was that influence which had, or would,
set itself in opposition to the souls remaining,
or the entity remaining, in that state of at onement.

815-7

Our physical body—our "suit of the soul" with its billions of atoms and light is truly a magnificently expressed Divine Idea. The body is an organism that gives "living souls" a vehicle for becoming conscious of who and what we are, as well as providing a means to gain information and knowledge of our physical environment. In fact we gain so much knowledge of "life in the earth" that it can often become overwhelming. Just think of all the things, ideas, people, and events that we have to label either good or bad, pleasing or painful, useful and useless, and so on into infinity. We gain so much information trying to create a safe place to block out our fears and all things "bad" and wall in what we label as good that we inevitably lose sight of our real purpose for having a body.

Through practicing spiritual disciplines such as meditation, we learn to balance our energies and experience a release from limitation, stress, and the many effects that materialism leaves upon the psyche. However briefly, we return to Eden to catch the sweet scent from the Tree of Life.

We meditate. We pray. We visualize and create affirmations. We go to workshops and classes, buy books, and listen to tapes—all with the goal of achieving wholeness, maximizing our hidden potentials, and releasing the power of the elusive 90% of our brain that our cultural mythology tells us is there and untapped. As each experience results in a little growth, our natural inclination is to make every milestone our CZ, or comfort zone. We find something and call it "good." And we think we've arrived.

Perhaps, that's why God allowed the serpent to have his place in Adam and Eve's perfect world. He wanted to make sure they didn't stay in there, because our current CZ is never the measure of all we can be or who we truly are.

Spiritually, no soul comes into material existence by accident. We are here for a purpose, and each one of us has a unique destiny to fulfill in our lifetime. We have lessons to learn, truths to assimilate, experiences to master, and challenges to face. Our destiny is to learn how to be Love, and we have the Universe's most compelling motivation to do so. We are designed to be the Image and Likeness of God, but we must claim it.

We pray for wholeness. But do we know what we are asking for? And what the requirements are? We want to realize our full potential and to grow into our limitless self, yet, at the same time, we fear those encounters push us beyond the walls of the CZ. Thus, we feel compelled to seek out experiences for growth, and at the same time we strive to avoid them. We are both compelled by our destiny and frightened by it.

Thus we find a curious comfort in the Known. We cling to it, even if it hurts, and call our Bad good and our Stagnation growth as long as it serves to quell our discomforts and fears. That's why Divine Mind in its Infinite Wisdom designed the Universe in such a way that we are constantly being tricked, enticed, seduced, beguiled, and cast out of our CZs. As the ancients knew, even in Paradise, there is a serpent in the garden—and it has its place, because only the Creator could put it there.

In the old fertility cults, the serpent was a consort of the goddess and a guardian of the sacred mysteries. In the ancient mystery schools, the serpent was frequently cast as an initiator and trickster. In later tales, a serpent/dragon guards great treasures—and must be tricked or slain in order for the treasures to be reclaimed or liberated. Only the tried, true, and pure of heart can overcome him. In other words, the serpent initiates a test of character for the aspiring hero or heroine.

Could this illustrious guardian of mysteries and treasures be the same one Adam and Eve found in the Garden?

On a historical level, the temptation of Eve is an artifact of the newly emerging patriarchy's successful attempt to disempower the old goddess religions. The patriarchy's revision of the serpent/goddess relationship cast the goddess, woman, or the receptive, passive, intuitive principle (Eve) as weak, unstable, untrustworthy and her potent consort, the serpent, as devious and evil. The success of the patriarchy, fueled by the evolutionary impulse of individualism, self-awareness, and self-identity, insured that this interpretation has prevailed for several thousand years. But we are living in a time when there is a huge readjustment in the cosmos taking place, and the feminine principle has reasserted its rightful and honored status in the collective mind. The goddess has returned.

Instead of a temptation, let's look at it as an initiation story. An initiation has to do with our willingness to be *awakened* by our experiences rather than karmically bound by them. In Genesis, the serpent is both an initiator and a trickster. The trickster is the voice within us that demands change. The initiator is the part of ourselves that knows our weakness and vulnerabilities and sets up our lessons to test our level of moral and spiritual development.

Eve existed in a state where she lived as a goddess, but she didn't know it, because it was her natural state. She knew no other. She was created in the Image of God. In Genesis 2, she, along with Adam, became "a living soul." In Genesis 3, the serpent "beguiles" Eve by telling her she can become like God. The serpent seduces Eve by offering her something she already is, but not yet fully aware. The voice she heard spoke to her true, but untested, unconscious self. And she responded, because the initiation was in line with her destiny.

Or, as Jungian psychiatrist and author Robert Johnson states in *We:*

> Until he (Modern Man) learns to confront motives, desires and unlived possibilities, he can never be complete or genuinely fulfilled. The force within which constantly urges us to experience unlived possibilities is the most awesome force—the urge for self-realization.

Edgar Cayce indicated that the serpent in Genesis can be understood as our ability to rationalize any decision we choose to make. Hence, the serpent, the devil, represents the power of that force of self-will misapplied, or selfishness. In other words, "do your own thing" becomes the ruling principle in our lives and the world— and we, as creative beings, continue to generate and rationalize a multitude of ways to operate independently of Universal Law.

As spiritual seekers, one of our most perplexing questions is, "Is it Spirit or ego speaking to me?"

Before her initiation, Eve lacked an individualized consciousness. The serpent tricked her into self-awareness. Beyond the walls of her CZ lay separation, the creation of a time-bound identity—the ego—and fear of annihilation, rejection, and abandonment. Having "fallen" into ego, the test for the soul now is to overcome its own creation—ego—and return to the Oneness with the Father/Mother Source, carrying the treasure of its own consciousness of the Source as its gift.

To become the Love we already are, we have to be seduced, enticed, tricked, betrayed, and beguiled from our CZs countless times before we can fully activate and integrate the Divine Image within us. Each time we find ourselves "beyond the walls" of our CZ, we have an opportunity to present ourselves for initiation. All evolutionary leaps are incubated in chaos and confusion. Every breakthrough is preceded by some form of breakdown. And a breakdown is simply a way of breaking out. As Marianne Williamson says, "Life is a gift, but growth is an option." The ancient Greeks put it more fatalistically: "Those whom the gods cannot lead, they shove."

If we cannot be motivated by the sheer joy of actualizing our spiritual identity and empowered by a passion for Truth, then the serpent—the trickster, the coyote—the undisciplined energy of the unconscious will supply the motivational keys to keep us moving.

SERPENT AS INITIATOR

In world culture, the serpent can represent the evil tempter, as it does in the Western Judeo-Christian ethic, or it can symbolize wisdom, enlightenment, and creative energy as it did in the goddess cults of the ancient world.

The undulating movements of the serpent as it crawls across the ground made the serpent an ideal symbol of the flow of energy waves, or life force. The fact that it shed its skin in regular cycles made it an appropriate symbol for regeneration, rebirth, and eternal life.

The serpent principle, as identified in the Cayce readings, is the energy that keeps us out of attunement with the Whole. Or serpent energy can be the very life force itself, which when channeled and elevated, creates enlightenment and unity.

As an initiator rather than a tempter, the serpent can represent that component of our psyche that speaks to our innermost desire, that finds words and ways to place in our consciousness reasons, justification, rationalizations to do what we want to do but are too timid, fearful, or too unconscious or too conventional to do.

EXERCISE: ENCOUNTERING THE SERPENT
Evil Tempter or Teacher and Guide

That [individualized] I AM is a portion of the great *I AM and thus is in consciousness for the preparation, for the schooling, for the gaining of that estate where curiosity, selfishness, self-desire is to be left alone. And in doing so does one become the more stable and the more honest with self. 793-2*

THE WISDOM OF THE EDGAR CAYCE READINGS

It was the eating, the partaking, of knowledge; knowledge without wisdom—or that as might bring pleasure, satisfaction, gratifying . . . Thus in the three-dimensional phases of consciousness such manifestations become as pleasing to the eye, pleasant to the body appetites. Thus the interpretation of the experience, or of that first awareness of deviation from the divine law, is given in the form as of eating of the tree of knowledge. 815-7

Selfishness produced the first self-consciousness— the awareness and pain of having an identity out of harmony with Divine Order. Out of pain and separation, the evolution and development of an individualized ego-centered personality with its unique history of choices and consequences began. The creation of individualized self-awareness was and is an achievement of a difficult and precarious evolution, and it is bought with a great price. That's why we cling so tenaciously to it and refuse to give it up.

Our destiny, as the readings so often emphasized, is to "be aware of self [an individualized portion of the I AM], yet one with the whole [to be Universal]."

That which we created is the very thing we must overcome—and spiritualize.

Selfishness is often a result of not feeling valued, loved, esteemed, cherished, or needed. However, a certain degree of selfishness is a requirement for survival and for mental health. We need it for emotional health and spiritual balance. However, the truly selfish person feels an emptiness inside and tries to fill that space at any cost, cramming in everything he or she can to fill the void without regard for others.

EXERCISE II: AN EXPERIENCE WITH THE SERPENT

We encounter the serpent when we come face to face with life issues. Life issues are developed as defense mechanisms from the way we met previous issues and challenges in our young lives. At one phase in our lives, the core of the life issue develops as a very creative strategy to insure our survival in early childhood, but as we age and mature, the strategy becomes a confining box reinforced by habit patterns, belief systems, and the fear of change. It becomes a "comfort zone" created with our defense mechanisms to protect us from the original pain at the core of the life issue.

A life issue then is a major theme in our life which challenges and tests us. Some major life issues are:

Abandonment	Rejection	Lack of Self-Knowledge
Guilt	Insecurity	Obsessive/Compulsive Behavior
Rage	Intolerance	Lack of Self-Love
Shame	Resentment	

IDENTIFYING THE ISSUE/NAMING THE SERPENT

The manner in which we experience our life issues and the way we name them determines which serpent we will encounter—"evil tempter" or "master initiator."

The test of personal maturity and responsibility is one of the major serpent initiations. And it challenges us through our ability to "name" our experiences.

We can say, "I accept responsibility for what I have brought into my life, and I choose now to change it." Or we can say, "It's not my fault—the devil made me do it."

If we can state the positive, then instead of "evil tempter," the serpent can begin to be experienced and understood in his more ancient guise as initiator, teacher, and guide.

Take a moment, now, and close your eyes. Take a few deep breaths and when you feel ready, recall a time when you felt hurt, wounded, assaulted, belittled, or betrayed.

If you choose, start a list and write out every hurt, illness, and emotional crisis that comes to mind—every disease, all your issues, every time that you felt victimized, cheated, betrayed, abused.

If you are not clear what the issue is, ask to be shown only what you are ready and willing to look at and work on now. Trust that your unconscious mind will give you the issue that you are ready to work on—not so large that it becomes overwhelming but not so small that it lacks challenge.

FEEL THE ISSUE

In order to heal it, you must feel it.

Close your eyes and imagine all the energy and negativity. Personify it as a serpent or any image that feels right for you.

If you choose, draw the image on a big piece of paper.

Now focus on the image and feel where in your body you have been bitten by the serpent. Where in your body do you feel its bite?

As you go within, allow the feelings, the memories to emerge. If you feel anger, act out your anger (without harming anyone). If you feel betrayed or rejected, release the feeling. Express it. Moan, groan, or whimper. This is not an intellectual exercise.

As you bring up and release the feelings, ask yourself—what have I learned through this disappointment, betrayal, illness, loss? What opportunities has this "serpent's bite" presented to me? What is the highest spiritual purpose I can gain from this experience?

Begin writing down in your journal the answers that come to you. Or, if you feel safe, share your insights with a partner or, if appropriate, in your spiritual support group.

NAME THE SERPENT

Now name the serpent. Remember, a name establishes the relationship you have with whatever it is you name. Will you name it "evil" or "initiator"?

Be honest with yourself.

Do you still want to blame someone or something outside yourself for the pain and misery you have experienced, past or present. Then the serpent is an "evil tempter" for you.

If you have gained spiritual insight or a new positive attitude from confronting the serpent energy, or if you now make a choice to assume responsibility for dealing with your own energies and reactions and raising them to a new level of creativity and wholeness, then the serpent will appear as a wisdom/initiator for you.

If you are unable to release the bitterness, resentment, blame for the pain life has inflicted on you, you are still stuck in a victim consciousness. You will tend to gravitate to the concept of serpent as evil tempter.

If you can look back and see valuable lessons, skills, depths, and abilities arising from your disappointments, betrayals, losses, hurt—if you can look back and see how these experiences broke down walls of self-protection and pretense and opened you up to experience more depth, more feeling, more of the ineffable mystery of life and love, then you can see the serpent's bite as an "initiation."

What have you learned, gained, lost, or developed as a result of your painful experiences and misapplications of creative force?

Name the serpent.

CLEARING THE ISSUES AND TAKING RESPONSIBILITY

If you want to explore further in this area, here is another exercise.*

Take a piece of paper and fold it down the middle to form two columns. On the left side, begin a list of every person or situation about which you have negative feelings.

On the right side of the paper, write out a list of sentences that start with the affirmation, "I am responsible for this because . . . " and complete the sentence.

When you have completed this exercise, you will be delighted by the increased sense of power and esteem you have claimed for yourself.

---

*This exercise is a modified version of an exercise developed by Brian Tracey of Brian Tracey International.

Our Destiny Principle

Let the training begin with that indicated in Exodus 19:5 . . . 4087-1

Now therefore, if ye will obey my Voice indeed,
and keep my covenant,
then ye shall be a peculiar treasure
unto me above all people:
for all the earth is mine.

And ye shall be unto me a kingdom of priests,
and an holy nation. Exodus 19:5-6

THE WISDOM OF THE EDGAR CAYCE READINGS

First, as seen or presented well in Exodus 19:5, there must be the desire for spiritual light, for spiritual insight, for spiritual purpose; that the body, the mind may be in accord or attuned to the Infinite—as manifested in the soul of the entity. 3685-1 When ye have righted thy mind to the correct thinking as to the Creative Forces and what they may bring to thee, study Exodus 19:5. 3684-1 To be sure, it is interpreted by many here that the Creative Forces or God are speaking to a peculiar people. You were one of them. Why not then, today? Although through the years your name has been changed, the soul is the same. Hence this is, as it were, spoken to thee. 5124-1 In application in self, ye will find that Exodus 19:5 applies to thee, if you wilt put away blaming others. Yes, ye feel aversions, ye cast judgments upon others. By whose standard are ye measuring thy brother? By God's love for thee? 3660-1 Keep the faith, then, in that which is so specifically indicated in Exodus 19:5—that is to thee, as it is to each soul who seeks to become one with the Father 3524-1 For all power comes from and through that Source. 3486-1

HEED MY VOICE

From "Let there be Light" to "Heed My Voice" is not a great evolutionary leap. It is translation of a spiritual awakening into a new way of life. As we begin to subdue the earth that is within us and put our lives in action in harmony with Divine Law, we must rely upon a source of wisdom and guidance that is beyond our own rational, but limited, self-centered inclinations. The foundation for this guidance is found in Exodus 19:5.

The loss of a comfortable and familiar CZ plunges us into a period of confusion. Confusion, chaos, disorientation, and breakdown are unsettling prerequisites to a quantum leap—or the "escape to a new order" when the old structures simply cannot contain the powerful energies of the soul which have been too long repressed or simply need a larger field in which to express.

Physicists call the brain/mind an "open system." Through the brain/mind system, a constant stream of blood, oxygen, nutrients, thoughts, information, and memories flows continuously. This flow of physical material and energy causes the brain to vibrate. Ordinarily the brain can handle the fluctuations and still retain its internal structure. The fluctuating vibrations may be felt as anxiety, fear, and uncertainty, yet the ego/mind is able to function as it normally does and still can make sense of the world.

However, as more and more energy begins to pass through the system, the strength and frequency of the vibrations increase to the point where the system can no longer handle the fluctuations. The brain is unable to maintain its internal organization or structure and begins to collapse or is destroyed. Even a small fluctuation can, in some cases, destabilize the entire system and push it out of the comfort zone.

The flow of energy increases with exposure to new ideas and experiences, with meditation, creative work, dreams, and flashes of insight and intuition. Things stop making sense the way they used to. Old paradigms are questioned. This expansion disrupts the whole internal organization of the brain/mind system. At this point, the system has an opportunity to move in an infinite number of directions, none of which can be accurately predicted.

This brain/mind paradigm is reflected in the story of the exodus from Egypt and the journey to Sinai. As slaves in Egypt, the Israelites were confined to a structure imposed by the pharaoh. Moses enters the picture, bringing with him new energy and ideas which at first the old order is able to resist. But, as the "plagues" continue, the old order begins to break down and finally collapses. The Israelites, at this point, are free, with a number of options in front of them as they cross into the wilderness. The direction pointed by Moses is one of them; the various rebellions (the golden calf, the constant complaining, the frequent challenges to his authority, etc., represent other possible directions). But the Bible is the story of the pattern of mental unfoldment "from Abraham to Christ," and Moses reflects that path of development in the transition of ego-authority (pharaoh) to higher mind leadership and spiritual integration (as leadership passes to Joshua).

Exodus 19:5 represents the introduction of an evolutionary opportunity following the breakdown or break out from a confining and restrictive comfort zone. Like the brain/mind, the Israelites had the opportunity to reassemble themselves by creating a new pattern, a new structure which could accept and process an increased flow of energy with less turbulence and fluctuation. But they had to be willing to "go with the flow." The entire nation had taken a leap into the unknown and was poised, ready to "escape into a higher order."

Cayce indicated that Exodus 19:5 was a good power point to reflect upon after one got one's own house in order. In other words, before we can begin to develop spiritually, we must take an inner assessment of ourselves, be honest about our motivations and desires— not to be in denial about what we really feel, think, and believe. When we know what we are working with—hate, anger, resentments, fear, doubts—and break free of their hold on our energy, one old system collapses, and we have the opportunity to grow in a new direction. Then it is time to claim the power points of the Exodus story.

Exodus 19:5 is the first message Moses received on top of the Holy Mountain after guiding the Israelites out of slavery. It is a message that is to be repeated down through the generations—a choice to move into the larger self we really are—or to remain trapped in victim consciousness and slave mentality.

Thus, the placement of Exodus 19:5 following the loss

of Eden in Genesis 3 provides the beacon light in the midst of chaos that points to an evolutionary jump. If we will listen to the voice within and become its nature, we indeed will become what we already are in the eyes of God—"a treasure" and a nation of priests.

The word "priest" derives from the Latin word, pontiff, which means bridge. A pontiff, or priest, is a bridge between God and human, between the spiritual world and the material world, between the unseen forces and the seen.

In *Anatomy of the Spirit,* Carolyn Myss, a medical clairvoyant and internationally sought-after speaker on spirituality and personal power, relates the seven sacraments of the Christian tradition to seven aspects or dimensions of personal power. The sacrament of ordination—the call to the priesthood—is symbolic of the task one is called to do in service to others. From the archetypal level, Myss states, ordination is the recognition from others that you have unique insight and wisdom that directs you in giving service to others. The sacrament of ordination symbolizes any experience or honor "in which your community acknowledges that it benefits from your inner-directed path of service as much as you do." It also implies that the value of your service is not only reflected in your profession or your calling as wife, mother, friend—but through the quality of the person you become. The value of our spirit exceeds the value of our tasks.

The promise is that as a priest/priestess—shaman-healer-bridge builder—your value will continue to increase in the eyes of God and in the hearts of the people. As a "priest/bridge builder," you will be honored for your wisdom, love, healing ability, problem-solving grace, peacemaking skills, or other treasured gifts that you express. And the treasure that you become continues accruing interest. It remains always in a developmental mode. Your growth and enrichment will continue unfolding as long as you heed the voice—and process the fluctuations as the flow of energy, ideas, information, and insight increases.

Once you are established in the conviction that a sure source of guidance and motivation is available to you, you are ready to move to the next power point.

Seven Challenges of Moses

The design for our spiritual growth is woven in the Genesis birthrights of Light, Divine Self-Awareness, and the Power of Mastery and Dominion. To make these spiritual birthrights a portion of our physical existence requires daily application and expression of these spiritual energies. The journey begins in Exodus 19:5.

As we move through the various power points, a transformation takes place. But, for the changes to occur, each stage must become an experience. As we apply Exodus 19:5 to ourselves, it represents the motivational promise of a new life once we have done the inner work of removing the binding fears and habits of the old belief systems and habit patterns that kept us in bondage, fear, and isolation from our true selves.

Slavery is a condition of being subjected to and dominated by forces outside of our control. Considering how often we "give our power away" through addictions, habits, fears, relationships, and selfishness, the shadow of slavery falls on all of us.

While the whole book of Exodus itself is a story that symbolizes mental development and the process of transformation and change, within Exodus are smaller stories which, like subliminal messages, reinforce and support the larger picture. Indeed, as sacred literature, the whole Bible is composed of many patterns within the pattern, cycles within the cycles that continue to enhance, support, and reinforce the overall spiritual goals and value of the message.

After the release from bondage, Moses faces seven challenges. The challenges are embedded in the story from the parting of the Red Sea to the arrival at the holy mountain, the message in Exodus 19:5, and the foundation principles of Exodus 20.

These challenges suggest dynamics we all face in the process of change, the completion of important goals, and the spiritualization of the ego.

THE FIRST CHALLENGE
Sustaining the Motivation

And Miriam the prophetess, the sister of Aaron, took a timbrel in her hand; and all the women went out after her with timbrels and with dances. And Miriam answered them, Sing ye to the Lord, for he hath triumphed gloriously; the horse and his rider hath he thrown into the sea. Reference: Exodus 15: 20-21

When Moses first challenged pharaoh, his only demand was for a little "space" to take his people into the desert to worship God according to their own tradition. Pharaoh refused, and the conflict escalated until pharaoh lost everything up to and including his first born. The death of the first born symbolically represents the total collapse of a pattern of condition. The chain of continuity is broken.

The Israelites, on the other hand, found themselves outside their CZ, in the midst of a wilderness, caught in a conflict between the conditioned demands of their habit patterns and slave mentality, and feeling the impulse and pressures of a newly released creative force that they lacked the discipline to handle appropriately.

Symbolically, Moses represents the awakened part within us which carries the energy of the Genesis birthrights. In our spiritual progress, when we have been sufficiently awakened within, the Will of the Spirit will take us out of former limitations and confining CZs into a new and expanded relationship with Creative Force.

The period when Moses confronts pharaoh relates to that disturbing time when we must get our own house in order—when we are sufficiently "enlightened" to know that the deepest and best part of ourselves is held captive by the ego. The next step is to raise enough energy and power within ourselves through prayer, meditation, right choices, and "naming" to offset the ego's force, and then, ultimately, to bring our energy to its highest level.

In our own lives, when we achieve a breakthrough, there is often great exhilaration, jubilation—a sense of celebration, excitement—as if now I can really get on with my life. After the parting of the Red Sea and the "swallowing up" of the pursuer, the people had a party. They were free of the "stuck place," and a lot of energy that was formerly repressed was released and free now to express. They joined together in song and dance and celebrated. After all the years in bondage, of feeling powerless and devalued, this feeling of celebration and liberation was a new and exhilarating experience.

Maintaining the joy, the sense of "We did it!" or "I did it, I did it," then becomes the first challenge.

How long can you keep your spirit up as you move deeper into your own wilderness experience?

THE FIRST CHALLENGE
Guided Experience: Miriam's Dance

As infants, we were born with a wonderfully flexible and supple physical vehicle. Without any effort at all, we could put our toes in our mouths. As children growing up, we possess boundless energy and imagination. And as we grow older—and less free—our minds, our emotions, and our muscles have become conditioned to limitation as our attitudes and thought processes become more rigid and fixed.

The purpose of this exercise is to explore body movement in a natural, graceful, easy way; to become aware of unconscious "holding" patterns that restrict natural, spontaneous expression; and to explore more open and expansive movements that dissolve them. We want to tap into the energy of "celebration" and allow it to move us out of old limitations.

Miriam's Dance can be done alone, with a partner, or in a group. All you need is sufficient space in which to move. Soft, flowing music in the background may also be helpful.

Seated on the floor or in a chair, assume a posture that

expresses confinement, restriction, imprisonment. Constrict your posture until it begins to feel uncomfortable, even painful. Then slowly, without rushing it, begin to "discover" that you can move. Imagine you are a sprout pushing out of the earth into the sunlight and unfolding, or that you are a blossom breaking free from the tight bud that held it in.

Open your hands slowly. Stretch and flex your fingers like a small baby awakening. Become fascinated with your ability to move. Imagine after a lifetime of being fixed, solid, heavy, immobile, you are just discovering that you can fly, float, glide freely. Flutter and stretch your wings—and become an Israelite crossing the Red Sea.

As you cross, with each step, with each movement, more and more of your old slave consciousness drops away. With each movement you make, you feel more and more free, more hopeful, joyful, optimistic. For four hundred years your people have been in bondage. All your ancestors have been slaves. All your life you have been burdened by heavy restrictions. And now you are discovering something new and totally different, something you have never experienced before.

And when you reach the other side, you are invited into the circle of dancers led by Miriam. They are singing as you join them. As you dance with Miriam and the dancers in the circle, you feel their exuberance and joy. Slowly you realize you are no longer hampered or oppressed.

Invite in the spirit of the dance. Allow the feelings of exuberance and self-discovery to well up and direct your steps. Move your body now in ways that seem natural and in harmony with your feelings of freedom, of liberating yourself from old confinements, real and imagined.

Through your gestures, empty yourself of old patterns and blocks and behaviors that have come through years of submission and domination and fear of powerful, controlling outside forces.

If you find yourself repeating the same gestures and movements, see how many new movements you can create. If you find yourself standing in one place, be sure to move around.

Dance until the music ends or until you feel "finished."

THE SECOND CHALLENGE
Transforming Our Bitter Experiences

... they went three days in the wilderness, and found no water. And when they came to Marah, they could not drink of the waters of Marah, for they were bitter ... vv. 22-23
Reference: Exodus 15:22-27

Joy and enthusiasm are difficult to maintain throughout the process of change, especially as unhealed parts of the psyche call for attention.

Three days after Miriam's party, the joy runs out, the dance is over, and Moses is faced with his next challenge—the task of keeping the people nourished and focused in a seemingly unsupportive and hostile environment. They enter the wilderness of Marah, and the people are thirsty. And Moses leads them unerringly to an oasis—of bitter water! And not a drop to drink!

Of course, the people protest. "With all that you've promised, if this is the best you can do, take us back to Egypt. We would rather drink freely of the Nile (denial) than die of thirst in the midst of this wilderness."

By definition, a wilderness is an uncharted, unknown, unfamiliar environment. Symbolically, it represents a state of confusion, the subconscious mind, or any venture into unknown territory. It represents a condition when what used to work for us—the known and familiar habit patterns and mind sets—no longer work, and to resolve our existential dilemma, we are forced to trust and develop a new way of thinking and being.

In the Scriptures, references to water almost always allude to Spirit. In other words, the people's thirst means that they have, in a very short time, lost their connection to the Source that threw the great party for them. Bereft of joy and energy—without a drop of water in sight—the newly liberated slaves are ready to abort the mission and return to their former narrowness.

But Moses is the superstar of water tricks. He has turned waters of the Nile into blood and parted the Red Sea. His task is to keep the party going. He cries to the Lord for a solution. God responds, and Moses is guided to a particular type of tree and told to throw it into the bitter pool. When he does, the water becomes sweet. The people drink, the flow is restored, and the journey continues.

The magical tree which Moses is told to plunge into the water is one you will never find growing in the desert. This tree has its roots in Eden. This sweetening tree is a reference to the Tree of Life, the most renown glyph coming out of Western esoteric, spiritual tradition. The Tree is composed of two pillars and ten sefirot, or centers of activity, and paths or lines of power which connect and flow through all ten centers.

The pillars represent the male/female polarity with the lines of power reflecting the dynamic energetic relationships between them. The left or male pillar is called the Pillar of Severity and represents the energy and principles related to form, structure, constraint, contraction, law, restriction, justice, judgment, and karma.

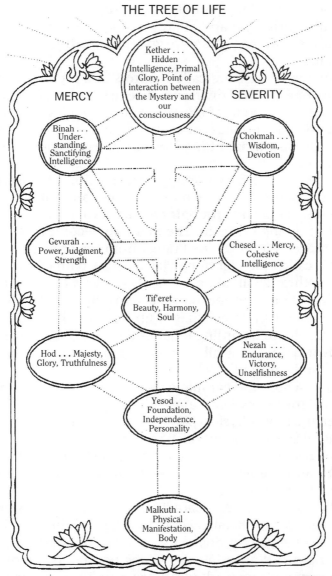

Sources: *The Mystical Qabalah*, Dion Fortune, and *Anatomy of the Spirit*, Caroline Myss.

The right pillar, the Pillar of Mercy, represents the feminine principle and energy and symbolizes expansion, love, mercy, grace, forgiveness, intuition, and dreams.

The ten centers are called sefirots and represent activities or aspects of divine intelligence. On the Tree they symbolize a system of energies and principles through which the divine ideas conceived in the mind of God become the visible manifested forms expressed and known in the outer, visible world.

At kether, the crown or uppermost sefirot, the divine Spirit is perceived in its most formless and intangible essence. At malkuth, the Spirit manifests in its most concrete and tangible form. The invisible becomes visible. The movement of Divine Energy from the crown to the root is called the Lightning Flash. As the path of energy flashes through all ten centers, it connects the two pillars in a state of perfect balance, and a third path called the Middle Path rises straight up from the Root to the Crown. Where Lightning touches the earth, heaven and earth are joined, and all the power of the Divine is totally and visibly present.

To be whole and complete, there must be connection and balance between the masculine and feminine, between the most physical parts of ourselves and our most spiritual aspects. It must all be integrated. When it is, we are healed. We walk in balance, and the bitter waters— the bitter experiences of life—are made sweet. We become the Tree of Life.

The Tree of Life as a paradigm of the Divine Mystery was said to have been given to humankind through the agency of angels, or divine messengers. In other words, the origin and meaning of the Tree lies in a realm outside normal human thought, yet can be accessed by contemplating the Image as a whole and the meaning and relationship of its parts.* The long and rich mystical tradition of the Kabbalah, of which the Tree of Life offers the most illumination, provides a system of keys to unlocking the hidden powers and knowledge of the Old Testament. It is beyond the scope of this book and the current knowledge of this author to present a more in-depth and comprehensive look at this multidimensional image.

It is offered here as a power point suggesting new directions and avenues for study and meditation for the reader and seeker for whom this image has inner resonance. And we shall soon see it again as our journey through the "challenges" to the mountaintop continues.

Our second challenge calls us to make choices— choices to transform our bitter experiences, to bring the energy of the Divine into those impalpable feelings and memories and transform them into sources of nourishment, renewal, health, and healing.

Above kether is the Allness of God that will forever remain unknowable and a mystery to the finite mind of man. The crown sefirot, or center, is where the finite mind connects to the infinite. At this level, the awareness is diffused and almost subliminal and incapable of being put into words. The awareness inspires an intuitive perception, and through this doorway the process

---

*Dion Fortune in *The Mystical Qabalah* likens the Tree of Life to a dream-picture arising from the subconscious of God which "dramatizes the subconscious contents of Deity." The Tree is an image representing "the raw material of the Divine consciousness and the processes through which the Universe came into manifestation." Since we, as the microcosm, are representations of the universe in miniature, the Tree of Life also applies to us and the processes which brought, and bring, us into being.

of bringing the invisible into the visible occurs.

After the old plagues of our habits, fears, and prejudice have done their work and our old internal systems have broken down, we are ready to break free of the "stuck place." We now have the opportunity to move in entirely new directions. A new vision of previously unimagined possibility and potential lies before you! And you have the gusto to go for it. Our next challenge is to ground the vision and make it real.

However, that initial enthusiasm and expectancy can carry us only so far. Soon, the wine runs out, and the party is over. Eventually we must begin work upon the neglected, rejected, and unloved parts of ourself that carries the "bitter waters"—the unpalatable memories, attitudes, and beliefs which must be changed. It is natural that once you peel back one layer of the psyche and heal an issue, you feel energized. However, as we heal one issue, another one is sure to follow.

When we deal with the issue that is closest to us, it allows other, older, deeper issues to come to the surface. Faced with the persistence and tenacity of these negative patterns, our energy will have a tendency to return to the old, established patterns and beliefs. After all, they are much more entrenched and established than the "lightning flash of intuition" which set you on your course and which is working itself down into your system. To keep it moving all the way down, you must sustain your motivation, rekindle it constantly through prayer, meditation, and acts of service and kindness, and transform the "bitter waters."

At this stage of the journey, the Divine does not condemn, judge, or strike down the complaining, balking, resisting Israelites. Rather, the Source feeds them according to their needs—first by transforming the bitter water, then by feeding them with manna, and then by bringing water from the rock. Later, after the message is given from the mountain and the people pledge to "hear and obey," the Israelites are karmically more responsible for what they know. Thereafter their balking, complaining, and rebellion is met with more immediate consequences.

Modern research suggests that the average person uses up to 90% of their psychic potential to suppress uncomfortable feelings and memories. In other words, we invest an enormous amount of energy and potential maintaining a status quo, even if it is uncomfortable, confining, restrictive, and unfulfilling. We are self-trained to return to what we know, rather than to move toward an unknown but hoped-for result.

So, recognize where you are. Notice your tendencies. It is perfectly natural that a part of you will resist, rationalize, and undermine the very thing you have set out to do. Be gentle with yourself. Listen to the voices that arise. Get real with what they are demanding. Feed them, but don't let them turn you back—or take control of you.

The second challenge relates to making choices to stay on course, no matter what happens or comes up.

GUIDED EXPERIENCE:
Bitter Water/Sweet Oasis

In a quiet, receptive state of mind, review your "bitter" experiences, starting with the most recent and going back in time to the earliest you can remember, knowing fully and completely that only the ones you are ready and capable of dealing with will come to the surface.

What are the experiences that you couldn't "stomach," that left "a bad taste," and were "hard to digest, hard to assimilate"?

Note them in your mind or write them down on a sheet of paper as they come up, even if they seem trivial, inconsequential, or you assumed you had dealt with them already.

Notice the feelings associated with these memories. Review your reactions and how you dealt with them at the time.

Now focus on the top of your head and visualize the crown chakra opening to receive Divine Energy. Visualize a lightning flash of energy flowing through your body, energizing all your systems, and then feel it rising up along your spine back to the top of your head.

Ask the Creative Source within you to show you alternative ways to deal with these unpalatable situations, past, present, and future. Notice the pictures or answers that you are given.

Give thanks to the Source for the help that you received and record your impressions in your journal.

As a composite image, the Tree of Life is a way of training the mind to see spiritual relationships using the "concrete" representation to think one's way back into the invisible or nonmaterial aspects of reality.

It is also important to remember that the Tree of Life is also represented in us or as us.

Using the diagram on the opposite page, begin to fill in the sefirot in the following way:

THE TREE IS YOU

First on either side of the column, separate your masculine and feminine components.

Put all the feminine attributes on the right. And all the masculine qualities on the left.

Now spend a few minutes and meditate upon the two columns you have created. You should have some feeling or relationship with all the items. Each item identi-

TREE OF LIFE: A PRIMER EXERCISE

fied is an aspect of your mental, emotional, or spiritual self.

As you meditate upon all the qualities, reflect on the idea that all of these arise from one single source. Reflect for a few moments, or minutes, upon the nature of that Source.

With a word or image, identify the "essence" of that Source and place it in kether, the crown.

In the top sefirot of each pillar, with a word or short statement or with a symbol, identify the highest spiritual perception of your masculine and feminine polarities.

In the middle sefirot, use a word, short statement, or symbol that represents your most supportive emotional quality related to your masculine and feminine polarity.

In the lower sefirot of each pillar, with a word or short statement, or with a symbol, describe the physical action or biophysical activity reflecting the representation of your male and female polarity.

Now at tipereth on the middle path, using both your knowledge base and spontaneous insight, create a symbol or image that represents your inner self—your soul or psyche. This is the invisible part of you.

Now at yesod, identify with a word or symbol a representation of your ego/personality—the persona, or "face," you present to the world.

At malkuth, using a word or symbol, create a representation of your body as the vehicle through which all of the above are processed and manifested.

IDENTIFYING AN EXPERIENCE

Another potentially fruitful way to work with the Tree is to focus on a situation in your life—a relationship, job opportunity, health or financial condition, or whatever you choose.

Make two lists and identify and separate the positive and negative aspects around it—both in terms of quality of energy, mental states, feelings and emotions, and physical manifestations.

Again, meditate upon the combination of aspects, positive and negative, as a whole and create an image for the essence, or originating source, and place it in the crown center.

Repeat the steps above. At the top of the pillar, identify the spiritual/mental understanding.

In the middle, identify the emotional representation for the experience.

At the bottom of the pillar, an image representing the physical manifestations of each polarity in the situation.

In the middle path—an image that represents the ideal outcome of the situation as perceived with the inner mind as it meditates upon the polarities.

At yesod, the face or appearance of the issue when both energies are present.

At malkuth, a symbol for the actual experience of the outcome when both energies are present and balanced and manifesting in the physical world.

Once you have filled in all the blanks, you have created a concrete image of aspects and energies both visible and invisible to contemplate and reflect upon. This image includes the elements represented by the words or images in the sefirot and the lines of power that connect them.

Reflect upon how they are all connected and how the energy has to flow together as one system to create a middle path. As you contemplate your Tree of Life, you may sense where one position feels weak or overdeveloped on your Tree, thus putting the system out of balance. Correct it with an image or word in the appropriate place that "balances" the system.

This is an exercise that you can use to sharpen your perceptions concerning yourself or any situation in your life. As you work with it, perhaps you, too, will experience the "sweetening" effects of divine insights.

THE THIRD CHALLENGE
Accepting Discipline, Following Guidance, Learning to Trust

Then said the Lord to Moses, Behold, I will rain bread from heaven for you; and the people shall go out and gather a certain rate every day, that I may prove them, whether they will walk in my law, or not. v. 4
Reference: Exodus 16:1-36

After the miracle of the sweetened waters and a time for rest, hunger once again stalks the Israelites. The place they are in is vast and empty with no familiar landmark or guidepost to orient them. The sacred mountain to which Moses is leading them is not even visible as a speck on the horizon. All they know is that they are hungry—and angry at Moses for leading them here. They demand to be fed. All they have are his assurances of a Promised Land ahead. If they don't get their needs met, they threaten to desert and go back to what they used to be.

How powerful our habits and appetites are—and how effectively they can limit the extent of our adventures when there is no concrete outcome or ironclad assurance in sight.

Moses turns to his Source, and the Source reassures him that the people will be fed. There will be bread in the morning. However, this heavenly food comes with conditions: they can only take as much as they need and no more, one day at a time. Each person is to gather only what is sufficient for the day. Each individual must now become aware of the measure of his or her individual need and daily requirements. The gathering of the manna forces them to become more conscious of themselves. It doesn't matter how much Moses gathers or their neighbors or anyone else. They have to respond to their own requirements and needs. If anyone attempts to bypass the discipline and stockpile manna for added security, the excess manna turns to rot overnight, and by morning it festers with maggots.

The purpose of the manna is more than just to feed them or teach them economy. It appears as it does, with its limits and conditions: *so that I can put them to the test and see whether they will follow my instructions or not.* (Ex. 16:4, New English Version)

Until we learn to trust that inner voice that knows our needs, there will always be lots of garbage to face every morning.

The miracle of the manna symbolizes another test in learning to listen to your own inner voice—the voice of your body, the voice of your mind and soul. It is another dimension of the task of becoming more conscious of yourself as an individual and not as part of a collective. In every situation of life—even in the most hostile, demanding, sterile, or difficult—there is always a sufficient supply of "spiritual food" to get us through if we are willing to trust our Source. Often we will find it in the most incongruous, improbable, and unexpected places, because it is everywhere.

Most modern schools of psychology agree with Carl Jung that present in every psyche is an "ineluctable urge" for self-realization, and this energy is seeking expression in and through us at all times. But out of fear and inertia, we often suppress and distort these urges. The result is we feel spiritually and psychologically undernourished and unfulfilled. Jesus said, "I have food you know not of," referring to His own ability to remain connected to the self-replenishing energies of His spiritual Source. As we become more aware of these bio/spiritual energies and processes and how they function, we can choose to participate more consciously. Then we can allow the "life force" itself to feed us.

In the wilderness, the manna was always on the ground with the first light of morning. In the Garden of Eden, Adam was asleep when God took his rib and fashioned it into Eve. Whatever processes produced Eve and the manna occurred during the dream time, the period of receptivity and repose. This suggests unconscious processes at work. When we awaken to the processes constantly working within us, we will find our "soul mate" with us and "our daily bread" spread all over the ground.

The third challenge is the challenge of trust, of knowing our needs will be met. Despite appearances, there are sufficient resources to carry you all the way through to the next place you need to be.

LOOKING FOR MANNA

As we set out on our spiritual journey, at times it may seem like what we are seeking is nothing but a "dream," a fantasy or an unrealistic vision or goal. It may start to lack a sense of reality, especially as old habits, old ways of thinking and reacting begin to assert themselves and demand to be fed. You may find it hard to keep going, that it is easy to be distracted by fears and self-doubt or worry, or you may feel disappointed and frustrated because some, if not all of the expectations you had are not being met in the way you assumed they would. But these processes can't be rushed. You can only choose to harmonize with them.

Take a few moments now to review and re-examine your past experiences where your resolve has broken down in the process of reaching important goals or maintaining high standards for yourself. What caused you to lose your motivation and the energy and power to sustain yourself?

Are you hesitant about committing to a high purpose or new direction in life because you are fearful and uncertain about your lack of resources, ability, or energy?

Remember, when selecting a new goal or direction in life, the important thing is to be realistic. Remember the pillars of the Tree of Life. The expansive and motivating energy of the vision and the dream on one side must be connected with discernment, judgment, plans, resources, and strategy on the other side. When these two polarities, or pillars, are balanced and connected to each other, they create a path for the lightning flash to touch the earth.

Do you have all the factors you need?

Are you giving yourself the time you need?

Do you have the proper support you need?

Is there anything you need to modify at this time?

Remember, the lesson of the manna story is learning what your own requirements are. If someone gathers more than you, don't judge or get envious of that person's portion. If some gather less, don't feel superior. Each gathers according to his or her motivation and needs. And that which is gathered in fear and greed becomes "dross" in the soul.

There is that of the divine within you that can and will nurture, sustain, and strengthen you in every phase of the journey.

EXPLORE

What are the tools and techniques you use to connect to your own sources of nourishment?

Reading inspirational literature	Working in the garden or on a craft project
Listening to uplifting music	Playing with my children
	Dream incubation
Meditation	Going shopping
Dialoguing with my inner child	Sport or hobby
	OTHERS_____

As an experiment, set a growth focus and dedicate yourself to using at least one or more of your inner attuning resources every day for the next forty days. Keep a journal, and make short notations for each day, and see how many sources of manna you discover during this time.

Here is one person's experience:

"I set my growth focus as 'becoming more conscious.' I decided I wanted to stop operating automatically from old unconscious habit patterns and emotional tapes. I discovered real manna by saying, 'Thank You, Father,' for all the events of the day that forced me to become more aware of my old tapes. This awareness expanded until I was expressing appreciation for everything—until I began to find reasons to be thankful for everything that happened to me. Some wonderful synchronicities began happening—the right book appearing, a telephone call just when I needed it—these became even more meaningful because I began to see a unity behind everything. They were coming to me as a result of my decision to uphold a growth focus. The Universe was responding, and everything was helping me grow. The real manna was my awareness of this. It was a persistent, constant feeling of being renewed and strengthened. I realized these feelings are always there, but I never looked for them before."

THE FOURTH CHALLENGE
Drawing Water from the Rock

They encamped at Rephidim, where there was no water for the people to drink. And a dispute arose between them and Moses. When they said, "Give us water to drink," Moses said, "Why do you dispute with me? Why do you challenge the Lord?" The people become so thirsty, that they raised an outcry against Moses: "Why have you brought us all out of Egypt... to let us die of thirst..." Moses cried to the Lord, "What shall I do with these people? In a moment they will be stoning me." The Lord answered, "Go forward, ahead of the people ... You will find me waiting there, by a rock in Horeb. Strike the rock; water will pour out of it, and the people will drink."
Reference: Exodus 17:1-7

After the miracle of the manna, the people once again become thirsty and belligerent. There is no water in sight, not even a bitter pool. The people mutter and argue and raise their voices in protest. "Why have you brought us here to die!"

When he was dealing out the plagues in Egypt, Moses looked like a hero and superstar to the Israelites. It must have been great fun sitting in the bleachers and watching Moses fight it out with pharaoh's magicians. But now the tables are turned. Moses seems only to be leading them to bitter waters and dry holes—and it's their turn to duel with him.

Except for Moses and a small handful around him, it doesn't seem to matter who is in charge or which direction they are headed, just so someone feeds them and sees their needs are met. The illusion of the wilderness is that it is a dry and empty place. The reality is that there is nourishment everywhere.

When the people project their anger and frustration on Moses, they challenge him by raising the issue, "Is God in this place?"

Undaunted, Moses turns to his Source—and it leads them to an old, hot, dry, sun-baked rock—and tells them to drink.

The fourth challenge is the challenge of the heart. The spiritual journey requires us to face ourselves. When anything within us grows too rigid, intolerant, or inflexible, it can only be a stumbling block and not a support.

A rock can connote cohesiveness, strength, stability, endurance. It can also be a symbol of stubbornness, rigidity, inflexibility, dogmatism, and resistance to change, as in someone who is hardheaded or with a heart of stone.

When it is open, the heart flows with the most life-giving, life-affirming vitality there is—the energy of love, compassion, understanding, and empathy. When a person builds a barrier around the heart and separates from these feelings, they become hardhearted and insensitive. Just as a mind can fossilize, a heart can turn into stone, as in "Pharaoh hardened his heart."

The fourth challenge then is to "open" our hearts to love and faith. God tells Moses to pick up his staff—symbolizing his power and authority—and strike the rock. He does, and water gushes out, and the people are temporarily renewed.

Often something really very physical has to happen to us—a loss, a disease, an unexpected disruption—before the heart opens. And if we do not allow these experiences to embitter us or take away our power, we can look behind these encounters and see it was no accident, but Moses with his staff, striking the "rock." Just how hard does he have to hit us before we shake loose from the old attitudes and fossilized mind-sets and experience the life-giving waters of love pouring forth?

There is a second episode regarding the lack of water and a rock named Meribah. This occurs in Numbers 20. The people again are demanding water, and this time Moses' anger soars to the boiling point when the constantly complaining people demand water once more. He takes their complaining as a personal affront to his leadership. Ignoring the "Voice" which tells him water will gush from a sun-baked desert rock if he will only point to it with his staff, Moses lashes the people with belittling words of condemnation and wrath. He makes a big show by striking the rock with his staff, and proclaiming indignantly, "Must I—*I*—give you stiff-necked and rebellious people water!" (v. 11)

By striking the rock, Moses grabs the spotlight and turns it on himself.

And, still, water pours from the stone.

He diminished the awareness of the Allness of God and drew attention to himself as the source of the Water.

And, still, water flows out of the rock.

Moses' most human reaction reflects an egotism that had not been purged from the psyche—a condition that would not allow him to enter the Promised Land.

And, still, water flows out of the rock.

However, had Moses had the patience to subdue his rage and point to the rock, the body-bound appetite-driven people would have been reinforced in the awareness that God was the source of their supply, meeting them at their level of need, despite their constant balking, complaining, demands, and doubts.

And, still, water flows out of the rock.

At the first rock, in the early days of the Exodus, perhaps it was necessary to "strike" the rock as a way to establish Moses' authority and credibility in the eyes of the people. Here was the leader who had great powers and could get things done. The Divine Intelligence in Moses knew that he had to "break through" to the people. But after the experiences on the holy mountain, the emphasis had to shift that God was in charge. That was a "hard place" not just for the people, but in this instance, for Moses as well.

GETTING TO THE HARD PLACE

The metaphor for the fourth challenge is "getting to the hard place" and the task is to make the "water flow" from the situation.

What is the "hard place" for you—the situation that most causes you to "shut down," "turn off" or that is your "place of contention"?

In what settings is this "hard place" most likely to appear? At home? At work? In close relationships? In judgments and attitudes about yourself?

What are you most likely to do when you reach a "place of contention"? Blame others? Insist on your own way? Or do you go within and seek a solution that feels supportive and creative to everyone?

In what ways can you "call forth the waters" of creative solutions and life-affirming values from difficult and challenging situations, challenges, and people?

THE FIFTH CHALLENGE
Confronting the Enemy of the Vision

Then came Amalek, and fought with Israel in Rephedim. v. 8   Reference: Exodus 17:8-16

The first enemy to make war upon the Israelites is their own distant cousins, the Amalekites, descendants of Esau, Jacob's twin. Perhaps the Amalekites saw this horde of homeless migrants as easy prey. Perhaps they coveted the well that Moses had opened up at the old rock. Or the attack could have been spurred from ancient jealousies stemming from the fact that their ancestor had been tricked out of his birthright by Jacob's cunning. But the significant thing to note is that the battle occurs—as it always does—right after the question is raised, "Is God in this place or not?"

The Amalekites are the ambushers, the saboteurs. They are in everybody's wilderness as the undisciplined, disruptive, negative energy lurking just below consciousness that is ever ready to spring forth and pull us down whenever there is a challenging situation to move through.

Whenever we lose or doubt our connection to our Creative Source—whenever we question, "Is God with me in this choice I made?"—in the effects it is having, in the direction it is taking me, in the situations I am experiencing—the "Amalekites," in the form of our doubts, fears, and lack of trust, spring out from their hiding place, intent on undermining or eradicating whatever progress we have made.

The great English mystic, William Blake, observed that those who are not willing to fight the battles within themselves are doomed to fight them without. Realizing we all have "enemies within," Moses' strategy for winning the battle with the Amalekites should be of great interest to us. On the occasion of this conflict, the ancient authors reintroduced the Tree of Life in a hidden way to reinforce the message that maintaining the connection to the highest source is the only way to insure victory in all of life's challenges.

When the Amalekites attack, Moses doesn't counterattack immediately. He waits until morning (a new period of Light). Then he climbs up a mountain to high ground, accompanied by Aaron, his brother the priest, and Hur, a loyal aide and warrior whom the readings indicate was also Moses' brother-in-law. Joshua, as commander, remains with the troops, ready to battle the Amalekites in the plains below.

At first, Moses stands on the high ground alone, with his arms outstretched. As long he holds his arms out, the battle goes in favor of Joshua. Whenever his hands drop, the tide turns and the Amalekites gain the upper hand.

After his arms dropped too many times, or he had grown too weary and realized he couldn't do this all by himself, Aaron and Hur come to the aid of Moses. They find a rock for him to sit on, and standing on either side, they hold up his arms for the rest of the day (symbolizing a full cycle of activity, or until the manifestation of Spirit is full and complete, and the victory is won).

With Aaron and Hur standing on each side of Moses, holding his outstretched arms, we cannot fail to see a veiled allusion to the Kabbalistic Tree of Life. The two men represent the two pillars, and Moses, supported by them, is "the middle path."

MOSES ON THE HIGH

Arranging the elements represented by Moses, Aaron, and Hur, the Tree of Life might look something like this:

THE POWER OF THE DIVINE

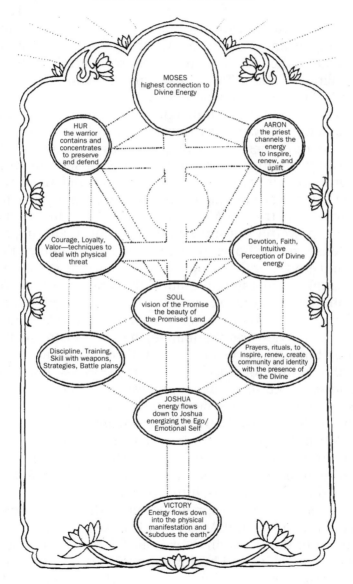

MOSES
highest connection to
Divine Energy

HUR
the warrior
contains and
concentrates
to preserve
and defend

AARON
the priest
channels the
energy
to inspire,
renew, and
uplift

Courage, Loyalty,
Valor—techniques to
deal with physical
threat

Devotion, Faith,
Intuitive
Perception of Divine
energy

SOUL
vision of the Promise
the beauty of
the Promised Land

Discipline, Training,
Skill with weapons,
Strategies, Battle plans

Prayers, rituals, to
inspire, renew, create
community and identity
with the presence of
the Divine

JOSHUA
energy flows
down to Joshua
energizing the Ego/
Emotional Self

VICTORY
Energy flows down
into the physical
manifestation and
"subdues the earth"

With the two pillars creating the field for the lightning flash, the divine energy travels from Moses, the head and highest point, down to Joshua (the Divine Image manifesting as an ego/personality struggling with an emotional challenge). The divine energy, carrying all the qualities of the sefirot, repatterns the emotional force and produces a spiritual victory.

The Middle Path, connecting Moses to the victory in the valley below, creates a Jacob Ladder of ascending and descending energies. As long as Moses remained in that position of attunement, his arms upraised and supported by his warrior and his priest/magician, he was the lightning rod attracting the powerful energies of the Divine. The triad of Moses, Aaron, and Hur functioned like a powerful transformer, or transducer, altering the intense cosmic power of the Divine into an energy that could empower the troops without "burning them up."

Unlike Moses standing alone, the three men created a stable connection and the newly commissioned soldier/slaves began to experience a transformation. As long as the connection was maintained, they were no longer victims, but winners, no longer powerless but powerful. But if the connection was broken, the troops—a bunch of undisciplined slaves in the process of transformation—were returned to their own resources and were no match for the "streetwise," earthbound Amalekites.

Moses had a strategy when he invited Aaron and Hur to join him at the top of the hill. He must have had a sense of his own limitations, or perhaps he was following some spontaneous, intuitive guidance.

When his arms dropped too many times, did Moses ask for help? Or did Aaron and Hur, seeing a need, respond to the situation? Was it hard for them to realize the great leader had his limitations? Was it threatening to Moses' own self-image to accept the fact that he couldn't maintain the connection all by himself?

What strategy do you take whenever you become aware (conscious) that a conflict, a battle is raging inside you? Do you tough it out for as long as you can, standing alone on your high ground? Are you willing to accept or ask for the help that is necessary to keep you feeling connected to sources of support and encouragement?

Do you have a "position of attunement" which enables the energies of the Divine to flow down from the high place in your consciousness into the valley below where the emotional conflicts can be won and the obstacles removed?

How do you respond when you notice someone is at the edge of their limits?

For a people who had been slaves for centuries, the victory over the Amalekites was a turning point. The same is true for us. Whenever we experience a victory over an old pattern of fear, a crucial turn in our attitude about ourselves takes place.

What are the victories over old limitations, inhibitions, and attitudes that you recall now?

GUIDED EXPERIENCE: MOSES ON THE MOUNTAIN
Your Position of Attunement

As an experiment with a "position of attunement," stand in the following posture and notice the change in energy as you raise and lower your arms.

We will call this position, *Moses on the Mountain.* Stand with your feet slightly apart and with your arms at your side. Raise them up slowly, outstretched, until your arms are just above your shoulders and below the crown of your head. Push your shoulders back slightly to expand the heart area. With your arms upraised, focus your attention on the crown chakra at the top of your head.

Imagine the center opening and energy pouring in and circulating through your system.

Now lower your arms. What do you feel? Is the energy diminishing?

Now raise your arms again until you find the position of attunement where the energy and receptivity are greatest. Imagine the energy as golden light circulating through the entire system, healing and repatterning your entire energy system. Feel it flowing through the chakras and going out.

How long could you maintain this position if the safety and security of your family, loved ones, community, or nation depended upon it?

Notice the thoughts that go through your mind as you explore this "position of attunement."

As we raise our energy to meet the tasks related to our spiritual growth, the fifth challenge is to keep our energy level up and sustain it. When the energy goes down, all the old "voices" and patterns that resist our progress reappear.

Regarding the Amalekites, Moses' charge was not just to beat them back but to eradicate them totally. But they turn out to be very resistant and continue the fight under many names and guises.

What is your "position of attunement"?

THE SIXTH CHALLENGE:
Reorganizing and Refocusing Priorities

The next day Moses took his seat to settle disputes among the people and they were standing around him from morning till evening. v. 13

Reference: Exodus 18

Moses' sixth challenge occurs at the foot of the holy

mountain. He has reached his destination, but he is unable to climb. After his brilliant string of victories and miracles, he has arrived but cannot go on. At the base of the mountain, from sunup to sundown and well into the night, Moses sits and listens to the disputes and grievances of the people on all matters, petty and grave, large and small, and dispenses "God's guidance" on every issue as if he were endowed with the infallibility of a pope. He is overwhelmed by the duties and responsibilities of his position as spiritual leader, spokesman, and "chosen" of God. And here, everything grinds to a halt.

At this crucial time, a key figure from Moses' past arrives—Jethro, his father-in-law. Jethro is a high priest from the land of Midian and was Moses' spiritual guide and mentor during his days as a shepherd after the flight from Egypt. Jethro sees that Moses has achieved the impossible. The Israelites are free. They have crossed the wilderness. And now they are positioned around the sacred mountain. Something great, something momentous is happening! The student has not only graduated but has surpassed the teacher! But the old priest wisely observes that Moses, for all his accomplishments, will never complete his mission without some help. Moses is wearing himself out—or fragmenting his energy, as we might say today, by overassuming his authority and taking on too much responsibility.

Jethro recommends that Moses delegate some of his authority to other "trustworthy" beings who could judge the multitude of grievances and disputes that arise. Only the most grave and significant issues should be adjudicated by Moses. This new restructuring and reorganization would empower and include others in the regeneration process and free Moses from the myriad pulls on his energy. "In this way," Jethro says, "your burden will be lightened, and God will give you strength, and you will be able to go on." (Ex. 18:23)

The Sixth Challenge relates to the sixth chakra. It is the task of keeping our mind and energy clear and uncluttered. At this level, Moses was challenged to restructure his priorities and formulate new relationships. He had to let go of his "superstar" image with solutions to everybody's problems and control over every detail and recognize the talents and abilities of others—and focus on his unique mission and purpose. Moses had to "recreate" himself in a new light—the light of the divine image.

The universe will handle the details if you are willing to release control and learn how to work with the energies. Keep focused instead on the attitudes, activities, and resources which lift you up, sustain your motivation, and keep your spirit lighter, more joyous, and less encumbered with the cares and concerns of the world.

Let the universe handle the details. Keep focused on the most important thing that you must do!

WISDOM AND MEMORY MEDITATION

On a large piece of paper, draw a circle. Or, if you prefer, close your eyes and imagine a golden circle. Now, in the middle of the circle, create an image of your "teacher." This teacher can be someone from your past, or a historic, biblical, or mythological figure. The teacher is someone in whom you have absolute trust. (On paper, you can paste in a photograph or images you find in magazines or books, or draw your own symbol.)

Imagine your teacher lives in the center of the circle. Now focus on the circle and know that you are whole and complete, just like the circle.

And then ask yourself, "What is it that I need to reprioritize and release?"

If you experience difficulty getting an answer, focus on the teacher and ask for his or her wisdom and guidance. The teacher's soothing voice and gentle wisdom frees your mind and you become clear and focused and in a state of inner harmony. New ideas, insights, and truth flow effortlessly and easily into your consciousness.

Now remember a time when you felt full of energy and enthusiastically approached an important task? What was it like? How did you organize your time?

Recall an experience when you felt indecisive, fragmented, and unable to complete important tasks or goals. What drained your energy?

Which way do you feel now?

What is it you need to reprioritize, reorganize, and rethink to get your energy back?

Formulate a plan, a strategy that makes you feel lighter, more joyous, and hopeful and less encumbered with petty concerns and negative energy.

Record your answers in your journal, and when you are finished, express thanks to your teacher, for he or she has come from the oldest, wisest part of your self.

THE SEVENTH CHALLENGE:
Reaching the High Place, Catching the Vision

Moses went up the mountain of God, and the Lord called to him from the mountain saying, Thus shalt thou say to the house of Jacob and tell the children of Israel.

Now therefore if ye will obey my Voice indeed, and keep my covenant, then ye shall be a peculiar treasure unto me above all people; for all the earth is mine.

*And ye shall be unto me a kingdom of priests
and a holy nation.* Reference: Exodus 19:3, 5-6

Acting on Jethro's suggestion, Moses enrolled seventy
capable elders from the twelve tribes and assigned them
the task of judging the disputes that arose among the
people. His willingness to be inclusive and to let go of
responsibilities and authority that were no longer suit-
able or effective for him to control released him to master the seventh and final challenge.

Now at the peak of this experience, having sustained
the motivation of the people, brought them sources of
nourishment, found his "position of attunement," overcome the resistors and saboteurs, and reorganized his
priorities to maximize his energy, Moses ascends the sacred mountain and receives the power point message in
Exodus 19:5. This is a momentous turning point. The Israelites are no longer moving *away* from a narrow and
constricted state. Now they begin the movement *toward*
a new and expanded state of being.

The Book of Exodus records three different ascents by
Moses to the mountaintop. The first ascent in Exodus 19
is described in a straightforward unembellished way.
"Moses went up to the mountain of God and the Lord
called to him." Moses received the message that if the
Israelites heeded the voice and kept to its principles,
they could expand and develop into something quite
extraordinary and become "special treasures."

Moses' second sojourn up the mountain is full of
drama. This occurs in Exodus 20. The mountain is
aflame and the air is thick with heavy, dense smoke. The
Source speaks with peals of thunder and flashes of lightning from the dark cloud. The people are afraid of the
power they see manifested. They step back, fearful that
contact with the Divine will kill them, and beg Moses to

step forward so they can get a message. Moses accepts and goes into that "thick darkness where God is."

The third ascent is recorded in Exodus 24. This time Moses takes Joshua and the seventy trustworthy elders with him. Halfway up the mountain, the elders experience a collective vision of the Living God "with a paved work of sapphire stone, clear as the sky" under his feet. Nobody dies. In fact they celebrate the experience with a communal meal. Moses takes leave of the elders and continues up the mountain with Joshua, his battle chief and spiritual heir, "and there he stayed for forty days and forty nights."

The esoteric tradition says that just above Moses, but out of his reach, hovered a great presence called the "Cloud of Unknowing." God was in the cloud, but there was no way for him to reach it. In other words, Moses did all that was humanly possible for him to do to connect with the Source. He had mastered six challenges and brought the Israelites to the foot of the mountain. When he climbed as far as his own efforts, power, strength, and will would take him—to the top of the mountain—the cloud was still beyond his grasp. There was nothing else he could do but to surrender to the situation and make himself available for whatever would happen next. He had to "let go."

Tradition states that Moses waited for six days and on the seventh day, the Divine Presence reached down and lifted Moses into the cloud. Thus the message was not the result of his own personal achievement but an act of grace, a divine intervention.

To be lifted into the cloud is to be taken up in consciousness and understanding that transcends the limits of our senses and intellect. As each of the seven centers are "opened" and the energy flowing through them increases, a new relationship with Spirit, or Source, unfolds. The seventh challenge of Moses relates to the challenge of reaching the highest, deepest, wisest, most knowing place within the Self and, in silence, allowing Love to speak. To hear it you must rise above your negative thoughts, the skeptical assertions, the doubts, and beliefs and let them go! These are the petty things that drain your energy and keep you from the "high/deep" place within you. When you can, you will no longer be reacting to something narrow and constricted—but moving toward something whole and complete.

A MESSAGE FOR ME:
QUESTIONS FOR EXODUS 19:5

What are the confining conditions (life issues) that I am moving away from?

What am I moving toward?

How is the voice of ego different from the Voice of the Spirit?

What processes do I use to separate and identify the impulse of the Divine from other beguiling impulses and conflicting urges that test my honesty, integrity, and ideals.

What kind of "special possession" am I ready to become? To my God? My loved ones? In my professional life? In my personal life? To those I interact with every day? To those with whom I have difficulties and differences?

What kind of "special possession" am I ready to become in my own eyes?

If you are studying this material in a group, how can you, as a group, begin to "heed the voice" in order to make your time together more spiritually constructive, healing, and strengthening?

Am I ready to begin?

GUIDED EXPERIENCE

Close your eyes and imagine yourself "heeding the voice" for six months. Now look back from the vantage point of the future. What changes have you made? How is your life different? What did you have to overcome to be where you are?

Now project yourself one year into the future. The inner voice is much clearer now. Your energy is stronger. Your trust level is the highest it has ever been. How is your life different? What did you have to overcome to be where you are?

Now project yourself further into the future to the very end of your life on your last day on earth. After a lifetime of "heeding the voice," you and the voice, with its wisdom and energy, are virtually one and the same. Looking back at your self now from that vantage point in the future, what changes have you made? How is your life different? What did you have to overcome to be where you are?

Now take a few minutes and record in your journal your vision about what the final result of this journey will be.

Initiation by Fire

... study thoroughly the whole of Exodus 20 ...

2969-2

The first seventeen verses of Exodus 20 cover the famous and familiar Ten Commandments; the second half recounts in dramatic imagery Moses' ascent up the holy mountain and two different attitudes toward God, one based on love, the other on fear.

As our spiritual awareness develops, we begin to organize all our experiences and perceptions around a central reality: everything that is has its origin in Spirit.

In Genesis, everything proceeds from one beginning—"Let there be Light." The regeneration principles of Exodus 19:5 depends upon one central factor—heeding the Voice. In Exodus 20, the principles in a blueprint for life and transformation come down from a mountaintop and are given to a waiting people who have taken the preliminary steps to free themselves from their former bondage and limitations. Now they learn it is more than their freedom they have earned. They have opened the door to unlimited possibilities.

The Ten Commandments represent a foundation for transformation.

In his little book *Metamorality* (originally published as *How to Break the Ten Commandments*) the great Unity teacher Eric Butterworth notes that a great problem we have with the Ten Commandments is that our interpretation and understanding of them no longer come out of the living experience of an individual. Rather, he says, the great spiritual principles voiced in the commandments have become encrusted with husks of tradition and dogma, institutionalized commentaries, and "stained glass attitudes and pious platitudes."

Butterworth suggests that if we are going to live the commandments, we must first learn how to break them.

In every spiritual tradition, in every breakthrough, in every path of achievement, there is always a strategy, a sequence of procedures or practices, that leads to the attainment of what is desired. There is a "way" to guide you to where you want to be that will sustain you through all your experiences.

The traditional, conventional, and institutionalized meanings, Butterworth declares, have created a husk which overlays the living essence of the Ten Commandments. The husk is a barrier that separates us from the living experience of the commandments. It also serves as a very strong container that enables the living essence of the tradition to be preserved and passed down from generation to generation. The commandments are like seeds, and when the husk breaks open, the vital forces of the seed are released and received by the seeking individual.

When we make the essence of the commandments a living experience within ourselves and, through meditation, reflection, and application, cultivate the nurturing soil which splits the husks and releases the divine energy of these principles into our minds, our bodies, and souls, what mighty forests—what mighty "patterns of growth"—will we give birth to?

Reflect upon this, and in your journal, draw a tree that represents what you shall become.

"MAKE IT AN EXPERIENCE OF SELF"

As we cultivate the Inner Voice through prayer and meditation, we soon come face to face with those principles which, for us, are life-affirming, spiritually correct, and most in line with our highest and deepest understanding. These are the principles which you must live by. The laws of Moses, one reading states, puts every problem directly in front of you—but always provides a solution.

It is of great moment to "receive the commandments." It is akin to an initiation marking the entrance to a new level of being, a new level of maturity and spiritual evolution and not to be taken lightly.

Before receiving the Ten Commandments, Moses told the people to prepare for three days. The mountain was roped off, and the uninitiated and unprepared were not allowed to cross the line. This suggests that not all people—or parts of ourselves—are ready, willing, or able to experience the spiritual energies raised up in meditation. We cannot take anything up the mountain that is not ready and willing to be changed. Otherwise, great harm can come. Make peace first with your neighbor, Jesus said, and then bring your gift to the altar.

RECEIVING YOUR COMMANDS

Make sacred space.
In what manner, will you create "sacred space" for the
Divine to speak to you?

Meditation	Spending Time in Nature
Dream Incubation	Fasting
Vision Quest	Forgiveness Exercises
Prayer	

PREPARE A PLACE

Altar
Medicine Wheel
Dedicated Space for meditation/prayer

How will you spiritually, psychologically, physically "rope it off" so that inappropriate negative influences do not adulterate your sacred space?

WHAT IS YOUR PURPOSE FOR GOING "UP THE MOUNTAIN"?

The two most important factors that determine the outcome of any activity you initiate are the intention and the attitude with which you begin it.

If you are seeking a clearer, stronger, and more direct contact with the Divine, what do you intend to do with the information, and what do you expect from it?

If you are indeed seeking release from any limiting condition, what are the principles you will live by to initiate that change:

Changes in lifestyle
Changes in the mental and emotional areas of your life
Changes in regard to the physical needs and health of
your body

What "commandments" are you willing to live by—
    for the next twenty-four hours
    for the next six months
    for the rest of your life
Write them down. Make a list.

THE TEN COMMANDMENTS

I.   Thou shall have no other gods before me.
II.   Thou shall not make any graven images.
III.   Thou shall not take the name of the Lord in vain.
IV.   Remember the Sabbath Day.
V.   Honor thy father and mother.
VI.   Thou shall not kill.
VII. Thou shall not commit adultery.
VIII. Thou shall not steal.
IX.   Thou shall not bear false witness against thy neighbor.
X.   Thou shall not covet thy neighbor's house, spouse, servants, or material goods.

The original laws were meant to be constraining and inhibiting; at a higher level, they were designed to offer support and direction for a co-creative relationship with Creative Force. In the original setting, the Commandments offer a set of guidelines that were designed to meet the needs of the Israelites at a level they were able to comprehend. The pronouncements by Moses were authoritative, dogmatic, and unbending. The laws were built like fences to hold the rebellious and undisciplined and unruly in check.

There is an interesting tradition that Moses received more than one set of commandments. The first set was given to him in the form of fire and luminous light. When Moses brought them to the people, they feared the power and the radiance which Moses brought down with him. And they rejected it, begging him to bring something they could live with. This light and power was more than they could take. Perhaps they felt unworthy or too identified with their poor, slave-bound self-image to relate to it. Or it forced too much rapid change. Or perhaps the teacher, in his passion and enthusiasm, gave his students more than they were ready to take in. In any case, Moses went back to the mountain and climbed the spiritual ladder that was thought to separate the physical world from the spiritual realms. This time Moses didn't go to the highest rung, but to the rung just below it, and talked to God. This produced a revised text, still reflecting the original pattern, but the power and light were diminished. This also was too frightening and unacceptable. Again and again Moses went up the ladder, each time to a lower rung until he came back carrying heavy tablets of stone on which were indelibly chiseled restrictive laws framed in the language of "don'ts." This time the law didn't frighten the people; it was close enough to their slave-language that it felt familiar and acceptable.

If we think of fire as energy and the radiance as intuition, or direct perception of spiritual patterns and divine ideas, we have a key to this story. The closer Moses drew to the Source, the more energy and illumination he experienced. On each subsequent rung of the ladder, the form and the pattern of the Divine Ideas or Spiritual Laws didn't change, they just took a different form—until the "husk" formed around them that virtually obscured the light and concealed the essence.

ONE STEP UP THE LADDER

As we reexamine the commands with the idea of removing the husks around them, one way to step up the ladder is to rewrite them in terms of positive, rather than negative statements.

The subconscious mind responds primarily to words and images that carry an emotional charge. *Don't, not,* and *never* are not emotional words, but words like *adultery, stealing, coveting,* and *kill* are. When we say, "Thou shall not commit adultery," our subconscious radar hones in on the emotionally charged words *commit* and *adultery.* Instantly, the subconscious assembles a feeling/picture created from the energy and associations we have with those words—and presents us with an image of a challenging sex object or sexy scenario to resist! You are caught in a struggle with a negative force generated by a negative image.

Focus your attention the eighth commandment, "Thou shall not steal," and automatically you have a picture in your mind of something you really want that isn't yours. The emotion is with the word *steal,* and to honor the commandment you immediately must struggle against the subconscious resonance it triggers. Lots of energy can be expended this way.

A more effective and less conflicted approach is to reframe the principles in a way that minimizes or eliminates altogether the conflict. In other words, honor the law of One by focusing your attention on the energy of the positive. Using affirmations is a very popular way to reframe and program the unconscious.

An affirmation is always stated in the first person. It is always positive and spoken in the present tense.

Perhaps stating the spiritual principles of the Ten Commandents in the negative mode was perfectly appropriate at that earlier stage of evolution and can be effective at a certain period or developmental phase in our lives. Resisting the negative force is certainly a great exercise for developing the muscle of your power of choice and will.

However, as many have discovered, it seems more effective to focus your mind and energy on what you want, rather than on what you don't want; to put your attention on what you will do rather than on what you won't do.

An excellent exercise is to rewrite and restate the Ten Commandments in the affirmative mode with no negative references. Develop ten positive affirmation/action principles that have applications in everyday life, and notice how much more energy and power these ancient commandments bring into your life.

THE FIRE PRINCIPLES:
COMMENTARY FROM THE EDGAR CAYCE READINGS

Edgar Cayce, like Moses, had the ability to climb up the rungs of the spiritual ladder to bring down new insights and perspectives that were a level or two above ordinary understanding. There is not a complete set of interpretations for all ten of the commandments from the Cayce source. Perhaps this is a good thing, because it leaves us to our own resources to search for applications and understanding and allows us to climb the ladder for ourselves.

In the following commentaries from the Edgar Cayce readings, you may find the "seeds" of new insights and applications of the commandments for building a new life and claiming the promise of becoming a "special treasure."

First Commandment

I am the Lord your God, who brought you out of the land of Egypt, out of the house of bondage. You shall have no other gods before me. (Exodus 20:2-3)

The Wisdom of the Edgar Cayce Readings

"Thou shalt love the Lord thy God with all thine heart, thine soul, thine body." If the activities make for the exaltation of the mind, the body, or the position, power, wealth or fame, *these* are of the earth earthy. Not that there should not be the material things, but the result of spiritual activity—*not* the result of the desires for that which the material things bring *as* power to a soul. 524-2 Do not forsake that first injunction, Thou shalt have no other gods before me, for in *"me"* is the sufficiency for the needs of power, wealth, position, fame, honor . . . For, when trials and turmoils come from within—with the abundance of this world's goods—there can *only* be that turmoil from *within* of a life not kept in attune with that injunction. For he that putteth position, self, power, money, place, before the God—*that* becomes the god, and must crumble before the Throne! 257-36

Know that whatever is good, whatever is true, whatever has virtue should be considered. Think on these things. For it is the purpose, the spirit with which an individual entity applies new knowledge in the earth, that governs whether such knowledge becomes good or bad. For, all knowledge is either put in reverse or is used as self-indulgence, self-aggrandizement, self-expression, without the thought of the first commandment, Thou shalt have no other God before me. Whenever there is put greater stress on one phase of a human experience, or one phase of any urge that may have to do with the soul, the mind or the body, to the excess of another, it may bring question marks to many. 3356-1

The God in self, the God of the universe, then, meets thee in thine inner self. Be patient, and leave it with Him. He knoweth that thou has need of before ye ask. 705-2 And if He comes and abides with thee, what would be the limitations? There are none, from the spiritual angle. And it is spirit—in self, in the Creative Forces—that will and does direct. 1549-1

In one commentary, the readings state that the "whole will of the Father" and the basis of all spiritual law is expressed in the commandment, Thou shall love the Lord your God with all thy heart, thy mind, thy body and thy neighbor as thyself. The rest of the Bible is "... *merely the attempt to explain, to analyze, to justify ... that saying, that truth ... "* (2524-3)

God is Love and Love is Light. Love and Light are at the deepest core of our very essence, the source of the soul, and every atom and cell of our being. In the beginning there was only one condition, one consciousness— the Christ Consciousness, the awareness of loving relationships:

The *Spirit* moved—or soul moved—and there was Light (Mind). The Light became the light of men—Mind made aware of conscious existence in spiritual aspects or relationships as one to another. 1947-3

The injunction to love God, love self, and to love our neighbor equally is more than a command; it is a memory encoded in the soul, waiting to be brought to light again by reclaiming our Genesis birthrights.

SECOND COMMANDMENT

You shall not make for yourself a carved image—any likeness of anything that is in heaven above, or that is in the earth beneath, or that is in the water under the earth. (Exodus 20:4)

THE WISDOM OF THE EDGAR CAYCE READINGS

To visualize by picturizing is to *become* idol worshipers. Is this pleasing, with thy conception of thy God that has given, "Have no other gods before me"? . . . Visualizing is telling Him how it must look when you have received it. Is that thy conception of an All-Wise, All-Merciful Creator? Then, let rather thy service ever be, "Not my will, O God, but Thine be done in me, through me." For all is His. Then, think like it—and, most of all, act like it is.
705-2

There are two parts to the entire command. The first is the injunction against giving inappropriate power to things, objects, and people. The second part of the command deals with the long-range effects of those choices.

In ancient times, priests and prophets directed people to be aware that there was only one force, One God, present in and the cause of all effects. To hold up or create an image and credit it with power was and still is a mistaken belief. If an image has power for you, it is because that object is a reflection of an energy pattern which creates and stimualtes a resonance within you. The use of an image to stimulate that energy is appropriate. To misidentify it is an error.

You shall not bow down to them nor serve them, For I the Lord your God, am a jealous God, visiting the iniquity of the fathers upon the children to the third and fourth generations of those who hate me, but showing mercy to thousands, to those who love me and keep my commandments. (Exodus 20: 5-6)

THE WISDOM OF THE EDGAR CAYCE READINGS

How is it given in our Word? That the sins of the fathers are visited unto the children of the third and fourth generation, even to the tenth. This is not saying that the results are seen only in the bodily functions of the descendants, as is ordinarily implied, but that the essence of the message is given to the individual respecting the activity of which he may or must eventually be well aware in his own being. That is, what effect does it have upon you to even get mad, to laugh, to cry, to be sorrowful? All of these activities affect not only yourself, your relationships to your fellow man, but your next experience in the earth!
281-38

The second part of this commandments calls us to consider the effect of our choices and decisions. How far ahead can you see regarding their ultimate effects upon your loved ones, your community, and yourself?

Abraham heard a voice. Something spoke to him, producing a sense of calling, of purpose, and he followed this intuitive impulse. When he died, he was a wealthy man, but not a great political or economic force in the world. Like the acorn, he was a spiritual seed which contained a thousand forests. He honored a spiritual impulse and made a decision to follow where it led. And with that choice, he set in motion forces that still continue to shape and change the world.

In the Native American tradition, decisions are based upon the the impact they will have through seven generations.

Do you consider the effect your words have on others as well as yourself? Do you consider the effect your words and actions will have upon your next incarnation?

Is there a condition you can identify in your life to-day—physical, mental, emotional—that reflects choices from a previous life?

What will be the consequences tomorrow of the thoughts you entertain today?

THIRD COMMANDMENT

You shall not take the name of the Lord your God in vain. For the Lord will not hold him guiltless who takes His name in vain. (Exodus 20:7)

When a sacred name is used for profane purposes, as in cursing and other forms of negative self-expression, it degrades the name and takes the luster from its holiness. This has an influence upon the person misusing the name and all others who hear it. There is a consequence when you secularize the sacred. You change your relationship to its power. You place it on the lowest rung of the spiritual ladder.

Life is holy, and the energy it takes to give praise or to curse is also holy. Our words are infused with creative energy that either build up or tear down, that weaken or strengthen. We also use holy names to invoke power through ritual, prayer, and supplications. If our motivations are for superficial purposes relating to ego enhancement, vanity, narcissism, and personal gain—then we are spiritually in error. The proper use of spiritual energies invoked through the sacred names and the power they carry is to give us strength and energy to perform service, to enlighten, ennoble, heal, and comfort.

At the "fire" level of this principle we identify and respect divine energy and relationships and keep to our true purpose.

FOURTH COMMANDMENT

Remember the Sabbath day, to keep it holy. Six days you shall labor and do all your work, but the seventh day is the Sabbath of the Lord, your God. In it you shall do no work, you, nor your son, nor your daughter, not your male servant, nor your female servant, nor your cattle, nor your stranger who is within your gates. For in six days the Lord made the heavens and the earth, the sea, and all that is in them, and rested the seventh day. Therefore the Lord blessed the Sabbath day and hallowed it. (Exodus 20:10-11)

THE WISDOM OF THE EDGAR CAYCE READINGS

Remember there has been given a law concerning how such days should be spent. Then know that love is law, and that law is that which may bring about the most necessary things in the mental, physical, and spiritual life of a body; for God will not be mocked by man's nor woman's own insignificant ideas of self's importance as to laws concerning the mental, or the physical, or the spiritual being. These have been set in, "Remember the Sabbath to keep it holy." Then *one* day must be kept in that way that will feed the mental and *spiritual* life of a body. All work and no play will destroy the best of abilities. Yet these have been set in the manner as is outlined in the *spirit* of "Remember to keep the day holy." 349-6

The allusion to the creation story in the fourth commandment provides, perhaps, a power point for honoring the Sabbath. How often do you meditate upon the story or powers of Creation, or reflect upon the source of the awesome powers, processes, and guiding intelligence that created your body and gives you life? Take time to reflect on Creative Power itself and on our place within the grand scheme of things. Certainly, using time of rest to point the mind back to the beginning and to our spiritual roots as the Divine Image is an ideal "Sabbath" practice. It provides us with an opportunity to refuel, refocus, and readjust our alignment to the Ideal.

Another method of observing the creation principle in Sabbath time would be to immerse yourself in appreciation of the natural world around us. It may have been just this type of meditation which gave rise to Psalm 8. And indeed meditating upon the Eighth Psalm would make an excellent Sabbath day power point.

Keeping a Sabbath rest restores balance and inner harmony. Too much preoccupation with our physical needs starves the mind and soul. The positive application of the fire principle is the admonition to respect, honor, and maintain your connection to your Source.

What is your way of honoring your spiritual self?

Of resting and restoring your mental and emotional self?

Of honoring your body/mind/spirit integration?

Is there a "Sabbath" principle you need to practice that honors all portions of your being and their needs?

Take a few moments now to renew your mind and spirit with a moment of thankfulness. In your own way, show appreciation by a word or gesture reflecting respect and honor to the source of your health, joy, strength—and your birthright of dominion.

FIFTH COMMANDMENT

Honor your father and your mother, that your days may be long upon the land which the Lord your God is giving you. (Exodus 20:12)

THE WISDOM OF THE EDGAR CAYCE READINGS

Q. *What will be the span of my life here, so that I may plan accordingly?*

A. One can make that almost what one wishes! . . . Some individuals hold that the day of demise is set with the day of birth, yet if that were so men would become only an automaton. But will and the purpose of desire, with the activities in its relationships to what has been the promise—"Honor—that thy days may be long in the land which the Lord, thy God, giveth thee," make for the setting of the time.

Then, as individuals purpose and make the activities of the life and the experience . . . more and more helpful, more and more beneficial to others, that promise becomes effectual in the experience. 338-5

How can a person honor their parents if they were absent, abusive, dysfunctional? This is the age of the "inner child." We realize we all carry a wounded child within us. Even the most dedicated parent cannot be present twenty-four hours a day to meet each child's perceived or real need.

If you bear animosity, bitterness, or disappointment from your childhood toward one or both of your parents for their shortcomings (real or perceived), how will you heal it—that *your* days may be long upon the face of the earth? Perhaps the wisdom in the honoring principle of this commandment recognizes that honoring is healing. We need to honor our parents, not for who or what they were, but because they provided a body for us and the opportunity to advance in consciousness.

At a spiritual level, when we choose our purpose for coming into the earth, we also choose the parents who would help us with the spiritual lesson of this lifetime. Each soul comes into the earth for a purpose, and the conditions that make up our birth environment and early childhood, including our parents, are of our choosing and essential to our purpose. Honor them for accepting you into their karmic field, and for the lessons they initiate for you.

To hold resentment toward your parents indicates you are resisting the lessons you chose at the soul level to honor.

At the inner level, you are the child of the oldest, or earliest, parts of yourself. Honor your origins; honor the "elder" within you that has seen it all and knows you best.

Who are the elders, the mentors, the authority figures in your life? How do you relate to them?

Consider what Jesus meant when He said, *For whosoever shall do the will of my Father which is in heaven, the same is my brother, and sister, and mother.* (Matthew 12:48)

The "fire" application of this spiritual principle might be expressed as "honor the active and passive energy dynamics within you which gave you life and which sustain you," and realize that there is only one source and that we are all "brothers and sisters."

SIXTH COMMANDMENT

Thou shall not kill. (Exodus 20:13)

The spirit of this commandment calls for us to magnify the life force in ourselves and in others. Jesus was demonstrating the "fire" level of this command when He said, "I came to give life, and life more abundantly." By encouraging joy, harmony, self-esteem, and other "fruits of the spirit," we are magnifying the positive aspect of this principle.

Spiritually, to "kill" is to deplete the energy in another. In a subtle way, we can "kill" when we fail to motivate and encourage others to be the best they can be. We kill with harsh words, criticism, ridicule, and verbal abuse. For most of us, the temptation to take a physical life is not a daily challenge, nor will it cause us to be more mindful of the impact of our words and thoughts upon others. And yet, in the life of the spirit, energy depletion—spiritual murder—is a constant issue.

In what ways do we kill the life and spirit in our children? In relationships?

What is there in you or others that you "murder" or treat with violence?

SEVENTH COMMANDMENT

Thou shall not commit adultery. (Exodus 20:14)

The positive observance of this commandment is to keep focused on the spirit and attitude of oneness and strive to keep your integrity and honor intact.

In what ways do you adulterate the purity of your intentions or the quality of your integrity and moral force?

In what ways do you "adulterate" the "voice" within? Consider the image in which you were made. How is that adulterated through the other self-images you have adopted for yourself?

EIGHTH COMMANDMENT

Thou shall not steal. (Exodus 20:15)

Stealing is taking something that doesn't belong to you. It can be goods, ideas, or nonpayment of legal debts. It can be done by not giving credit where credit is due. We steal by denying opportunity to another, thus robbing someone of his or her chance to develop, express, or advance. A teacher who isn't committed to her students robs them of their opportunity to learn.

The "fire" application of this commandment is to develop a prosperity consciousness and an attitude of abundance and to share it generously with others.

You steal from yourself by looking for easy ways out of difficult situations.

By not being honest or dealing directly with your own feelings, you rob the "spiritual seed" within you of vital nutrients for maturity and spiritual and emotional growth.

NINTH COMMANDMENT

Thou shall not bear false witness against thy neighbor. (Exodus 20:16)

The positive aspect of this command is to look through

the illusions and projections in order to to behold the
divine image and potential in yourself and others.

One of the most beautiful and compelling examples
of giving "true witness" was voiced by Nelson Mandela
in his 1994 inaugural speech as president of South Africa.

> Our deepest fear is not that we are inadequate.
> Our deepest fear is that we are powerful beyond
> measure. It is our Light not our darkness that most
> frightens us. We ask ourselves who am I to be bril-
> liant, gorgeous, talented, and fabulous? Actually,
> who are you not to be? You are a child of God. Your
> playing small doesn't serve the world. There's noth-
> ing enlightened about shrinking so that other
> people won't feel insecure around you. We were
> born to make manifest the Glory of God within us.
> It's not just in some of us, it's in every one. And as
> we let our own Light shine, we unconsciously give
> other people permission to do the same. And as we
> are liberated from our own fear, our presence auto-
> matically liberates others.

Do you look for the best in people? Or try to find what
is positive, constructive, helpful, and supportive in relationships?

Does your manner of being encourage people to be
open and truthful? Or must they bear "false witness" to
protect themselves from your hostility, reactiveness, and
power-tripping?

When we negate ourselves in our own consciousness,
we are bearing false witness to the Divine Within.

TENTH COMMANDMENT

You shall not covet your neighbor's house; you shall not covet your neighbor's wife, nor his male servant, nor his female servant, nor his ox, nor his donkey, nor anything that is your neighbor's. (Exodus 20:17)

Coveting is similar to stealing. Our energy is focused on what belongs to others, rather than on using our own resources to build up our own consciousness and abilities to gain and attract to us what is ours.

To honor this commandment, focus your energy on your own development and celebrate the achievement of others. Use the prosperity of others as a model for your own potential. Harbor no jealousy or resentment. Send out blessings and appreciation to others who seem to have what you want. Bless them for they are showing you what's humanly possible to have and achieve. By blessing them you open a way for the energy of prosperity to flow through you and attract to you the possessions you require to fulfill your purpose and learn your life lessons.

THE TREE OF LIFE
AND
THE FIRE PRINCIPLES

I. THOU SHALL HAVE NO OTHER GODS BEFORE ME.
The God in self, the God of the universe, then, meets thee in thine inner self. 705-2
Recognize the Spirit within.

II. THOU SHALL NOT MAKE ANY GRAVEN IMAGES.
For he that putteth position, self, power, money, place, be-

fore the God—that *becomes the god, and must crumble before the Throne! 257-36*
Keep your power intact.

III.   THOU SHALL NOT TAKE THE NAME OF THE LORD IN VAIN.
Identify and respect divine energy and relationships.

IV.   REMEMBER THE SABBATH DAY.
All work and no play will destroy the best of abilities. Yet these have been set in the manner as is outlined in the spirit *of "Remember to keep the day holy." 349-6*
Respect and maintain your connection to the Divine Source.

V.   HONOR THY FATHER AND MOTHER.
Then, as individuals purpose and make the activities of the life and the experience . . . more and more helpful, more and more beneficial to others, that promise becomes effectual in the experience. 338-5
Honor equally the active and passive polarities that gave you life and sustain you.

VI.   THOU SHALL NOT KILL.
Affirm life, joy, creativity, beauty, and harmony in yourself and others.

VII.   THOU SHALL NOT COMMIT ADULTERY.
Keep focused on oneness and your integrity.

VIII.   THOU SHALL NOT STEAL.
Develop a prosperity consciousness and an attitude of abundance and supply.

IX.   THOU SHALL NOT BEAR FALSE WITNESS AGAINST THY NEIGHBOR.
See through the illusions and projections and behold the Divine Image in others.

X. THOU SHALL NOT COVET THY NEIGHBOR'S
     HOUSE, SPOUSE, SERVANTS, OR MATERIAL
     GOODS.
Focus your desires on your own development and celebrate the achievement of others.

Rather than seeing the Ten Commandments as separate laws, picture them as elements of a complete system—configurations of activity and energy that manifest
as complete representations of the Divine Image.

The divine power transmitted through these archetypal energy patterns goes through the soul and into our
biology. We become the Tree of Life. Each principle is a
branch of the tree, and when all ten centers are active
and flowing as a single system, each branch is ever
blooming. Jesus' parable of the vine and the branches in
John 15 has relevance to this image. Pay special attention to His stated reason for sharing the parable: "I tell
you this, that your joy may be full." (John 15:11)

Perhaps the commandments, representing an entire
energy system at the "fire" level of divine perception was
the gift that became available to Moses by completing
the seven challenges. It is up to us to take the "tablets of
stone," connoting heaviness and restriction, and raise
them up until they become fire and light for us.

Exodus 20: The Second Half

*Now when all the people perceived the thunderings and the
lightnings and the sound of the trumpet and the mountains
were smoking, the people were afraid and trembled; and they
stood afar off, and said to Moses, "You speak to us, and we will
hear: but let not God speak to us lest we die."*

(Exodus 20:18-19)

WISDOM FROM THE EDGAR CAYCE READINGS

"Ah," ye say, "but many are not able to speak to God!" Many, you say are fearful. Why? Have ye gone so far astray that ye cannot approach Him who is all merciful? He knows thy desires and thy needs, and can only supply according to the purposes that ye would perform within thine own self . . .

If any of you say, "Yes, but it was spoken to those of old—we have no part in such," then indeed ye have no part. They that would know God, would know their own souls, would know how to meditate or talk with God, must believe that He *is*—and that He rewards those who seek to know and to do His biddings.

That He gave of old is as new today as it was in the beginning of man's relationship or seeking to know the will of God, if ye will but call on Him *within* thine inner *self!* Know that thy body is the temple of the living God. *There* He has promised to meet thee! . . .

Then, woe be unto thee—lest ye set thy house in order.

281-41

STUDY THOROUGHLY THE WHOLE OF EXODUS 20

The second half of Exodus 20 presents one of the most vivid and compelling images of the Old Testament. A large mass of newly freed slaves are cowering at the foot of a smoking, quaking sacred mountain. The God of their ancestors, whom they have known only through their oral traditions passed down from generation to generation, is now fully present and shaking the ground. Fearful that direct contact with such a powerful force is fatal, they beseech their leader to go up the mountain and bring back a message to them. In return, they promise to listen and obey. Then, as told in one of the great evocative, unforgettable lines of the Bible, Moses ascends the mountain and "goes into that thick darkness where God is."

In the practice of meditation, or in any experience where we confront divine truth, this graphic picture becomes our own story. Old parts of ourselves actually do "die" as we raise the divine energy up in meditation. The "divine radiant inner fire" of the spirit, when released, burns up the negativity we have stored in ourselves. Of course, the ego-based, fearful, selfish parts of us resist confronting truth in any form, because in the presence of truth they die.

When we lose these old familiar, fear-based, selfish parts of ourselves, it can raise all the emotions of a death experience. However, before we can make room for the new, higher order of being within ourselves, the old clutter must be cleaned out. Old familiar and habitual patterns of consciousness and self-identity must be released if the higher vibrations of spirit are to flow through the system.

QUESTIONS FOR MEDITATION

What is it that I have to give up or "let die" within me to have a clearer and more complete relationship with God (or whatever I call my concept of God)? What do I imagine would come in its place?

What is my greatest expectation in knowing God?

What is my greatest fear in knowing God?

The Great Chapter

In the 30th of Deuteronomy find what is told thee—
thee—to do! 262-121

DEUTERONOMY 30

*Now it shall come to pass when all these things come upon
you, the blessings and the curses which I have set before you,
and you call them to mind among all the nations where the
Lord your God drives you. (v. 1)*

*And you return to the Lord your God and obey His voice,
according to all that I command you today, you and your children, with all your heart and all your soul, (v. 2)*

*that the Lord will bring you back from captivity and have
compassion on you and gather you again from all the nations
where the Lord your God has scattered you. (v. 3)*

*If any of you are driven out to the farther parts under heaven,
from there the Lord your God will gather you, and from there
He will bring you. (v. 4)*

*The Lord your God will bring you to the land which your
fathers possessed, and you shall possess it. He will prosper you*

and multiply you more than your fathers. (v. 5)

And the Lord your God will circumcise your heart and the heart of your descendants, to love the Lord your God with all your heart and with all your soul, that you may live. (v. 6)

Also the Lord your God will put all these curses on your enemies and on those who hate you, who persecuted you. (v. 7)

And you will again obey the voice of the Lord and do all His commandments which I command you today. (v. 8)

And the Lord your God will make you abound in all the work of your hand, in the fruit of your body, in the increase of your livestock, and in the produce of your land for good, for the Lord will again rejoice over you for good as He rejoiced over your Fathers, (v. 9)

if you obey the voice of the Lord your God to keep His commandments and His statutes which are written in this book of the Law and if you turn to the Lord your God with all your heart and with all your soul. (v. 10)

INTRODUCTION

Deuteronomy 30 is the "great" chapter of the Old Testament. In the more than 14,000 Edgar Cayce readings, Deuteronomy 30 is the most often quoted and recommended Old Testament verse. Frequently it was recommended to be studied with Exodus 19:5 to reinforce the assurance of the nearness of God's Voice. And with even more regularity, it was coupled with recommendations to be studied and compared with Jesus' last discourse in John 14-17.

Deuteronomy 30 is Moses' last words to his people—to us. They are the conclusions, the understandings he has evolved, matured into and grown into after 120 years of seeking God and giving service to his people.

This, then, is all-inclusive, yet may be better discerned in the study and the application of the tenets set in the thirtieth (30th) of Deuteronomy by the lawgiver in his admonition, in his summing up of the laws, the ordinances that had been indicated *for a peculiar people, set aside for a purpose—as a channel through which there might be the discerning of the spirit made manifest in flesh.* [author's italics]

2879-1

HEED THE VOICE

In the Jan./Feb. 1995 issue of *Venture Inward,* an inspiring account is given of one man's recovery from Lou Gehrig's disease, a deadly affliction with no known allopathic cure. The first step toward recovery for David Atkinson began with the only reading Edgar Cayce gave for Lou Gehrig's disease and, as David states, a kick in the pants from Moses.

The first thing I saw in the reading was, "Do the first things first. Begin with reading Exodus 19:5 and Deuteronomy 30. Apply these to self" ... And when I saw that the two recommendations were Scriptures, I said, "Now I know this is hocus pocus" ... When I kept getting worse and the doctors said there was nothing they could do, I got the reading out again and read it over for several days, and finally decided to read those chapters in the Bible.

Deuteronomy 30 hit me like a brick, because it's where Moses tells you, point blank, how you can have good health and live, or how you can be sick ... And it struck me so that I read it over and over again. My lifestyle, my non-relation to Him put me in a category that was described in Deuteronomy 30.*

---

*See "Winning over Lou Gehrig's Disease," p. 20.

The impact of these power points from Moses motivated David to begin a spiritual search and a change in lifestyle. For the first time in twenty years, he went to church, and among the other blessings he discovered was the love and support of a caring community—an essential ingredient present in virtually all reported cases of "remarkable recoveries."

The encouraging outcome motivated David to follow additional recommendations in the reading, recommendations which he had considered "too far out," but when applied diligently and faithfully led the way to a complete recovery.

Now as we turn to this great chapter, let's open our ears and hear what these verses tell us to do!

THE FIRST TEN VERSES

The primary emphasis on the first ten verses is on remembering to heed the voice—the voice within.

When this inner voice is faithfully honored, our Genesis birthrights will be fully restored. Abundance and prosperity are affirmed and the inheritance of a perfected "ground of being"—a Promised Land—is assured.

In these first ten verses, nine different cause-and-effect relationships are identified:

Verses 1-4 *Heed the voice*—and experience release from whatever bondage or "stuck place" you find yourself in.

Heed the voice—and you will experience Divine Force as compassionate and personal rather that punishing and remote.

Heed the voice—and you will be restored to a state of inner unity and harmony ("gathered back") from whatever fragmented or "far out" physical, psychological, or spiritual condition you have moved into.

Verse 5 —*Heed the voice*—and you will gain access to the oldest, most generative powers in the Universe—and will grow beyond your expectations.

Verse 6 —*Heed the voice*—and you will experience a more profound and satisfying relationship with your Creative Source. You and all you generate will be infused with a loving, dynamic appreciation of the Divine.

Verse 7—*Heed the voice*—and in your new relationship with Creative Energy, you will experience immunity from the effects of negative vibrations.

Verses 8 and 9—*Heed the voice*—and there will be a growth of eagerness and desire to follow the prompting of the inner voice, and as a result you will grow in health, ability, and personal power.

Verse 10 —*Heed the voice*—and know that to realize these blessings, you must commit all of your body, mind, and soul unconditionally to the process!

Like all the verses of this study, Deuteronomy 30 is not a history lesson but a series of principles that are meant to be lived and applied. The principles are stated in terms of images and symbols that were relevant for people of a certain environment and historical time. However, like our dreams, the Bible, whether in English, Hebrew, French, or Swahili, is still written in the language of images and symbols. And through the images and symbols, we connect to the energy of their source.

Symbols are the doorways to the unconscious and always point to something beyond themselves.

A MESSAGE FOR ME:

Listening for the message of Deuteronomy 30 is a way

of looking deeper and "interpreting" in terms that fit your personal experience.

> *Now it shall come to pass when all these things come upon you, the blessings and the curses which I have set before you and you call them to mind among all the nations where the Lord your God drives you. (v. 1)*

Wherever I find myself, that is where I must begin. After I have had my share of success and failures, glories and shame, and I begin to realize there is more to life than this endless round of highs and lows, blessings and curses, successes and failures, wherever I am is where I must start.

To be called back from whatever nation I find myself in means to me I will no longer be governed by inherited states of consciousness or conditions of the "mass mind." I will slowly awaken into a personal unique relationship with God and begin to understand the consequences of my choices.

> *And you return to the Lord your God and obey His voice, according to all that I command you today, you and your children, with all your heart and all your soul . . . (v. 2)*

This is the greatest challenge, honoring the Voice within—and honoring it in the now, "today" in the only time that is. The meaning of *with all your heart and all your soul* is apparent. All my resources and energy must be committed to the task of living in harmony with Divine Law, with the spirit of truth. It must be my top priority! *"Seek first the kingdom, and all else will be added unto thee."*

... that the Lord will bring you back from captivity and have compassion on you and gather you again from all the nations where the Lord your God has scattered you. (v. 3)

What is captivity? Name your captivity—the life issues, the conditions that have you confined to the limitations of your sense-bound consciousness. There are many, many forms of bondage. The greatest of these is "self"—selfishness. The message is that when we begin to remember and apply, our experience of the Divine will changes. It will no longer be a distant and remote source, or a punishing and incomprehensible one, but rather we will begin to experience it consistently as a loving, warm, compassionate, and caring source.

... and gather you again from all the nations where the Lord your God has scattered you. (v. 3)

This verse can also mean that as I listen to the "voice within" I will be drawn into relationships with people of diverse backgrounds, experiences, social positions, etc., who also are heeding the voice. We will discover we are the nation of Oneness, a spiritual nation of priests/ bridge builders. We will no longer be limited, confined, or defined to the "nation" of our birth and upbringing— the collective mentality of our ethnic origins, religious upbringing, economic, or social status or any other group mind that governs our activity. We will respond to the Divine Within. *"The words I speak are the Father's; He does the works."*

If any of you are driven out to the farther parts under heaven, from there the Lord your God will gather you, and from there He will bring you. (v. 4)

Heaven is where God is—and there is no place where God is not. But to be in the "farther parts" means to be away from the center, away from a condition and consciousness of wholeness and relatedness to the ultimate good, God. Even when we have gone to the farthest edges—into psychosis, breakdown, abnormal behavior—we will be healed and brought to wholeness as we begin to "heed the Light" and remember who we really are—the divine image.

The Lord your God will bring you to the land which your fathers possessed, and you shall possess it. (v. 5)

References to "fathers" are very potent because of our feelings and relationship to our natural fathers, many of whom may have been absent, dysfunctional, or inadequate. However, the more removed from the present the fathers are, the greater our tendency to mythologize and idealize them. Our fathers of the remote past were giants, gods, and heroes. They belong to the land of the soul, the psyche, the ground of our being.

He will prosper you and multiply you more than your fathers. (v. 5)

Rather than looking back to role models and hero figures, I will become content and empowered by my own accomplishments and experiences as I put into practice the prompting and guidance from the "Voice" of the Light within. Consider the promise of Jesus: "*Greater things than these, you shall do, because I go to my Father.*"

And the Lord your God will circumcise your heart and the heart of your descendants, to love the Lord

your God with all your heart and with all your soul,
that you may live. (v. 6)

Isn't this a lovely verse! As we "heed the voice" and "remember the Light," we shall become more sensitive, caring, and *alive!*

Also the Lord your God will put all these curses on
your enemies and on those who hate you, who perse-
cuted you. (v. 7)

Those who persecute someone who is in harmony with Divine Purpose and Law will have their own actions, thoughts, and hostility turned back on them!

And you will again obey the voice of the Lord and
do all His commandments which I command you
today. (v. 8)

And the natural result of seeing all these principles working out will be a stronger motivation and intent to continue walking the path of the Awakening.

. . . the Lord your God will make you abound in all
the work of your hand, in the fruit of your body, in
the increase of your livestock, and in the produce of
your land for good . . . (v. 9)

The blessings will multiply on every level. Look forward to fullness and joy, productivity and purpose on all levels, in all areas of life. (See also Psalm 1.)

for the Lord will again rejoice over you for good as
He rejoiced over your Fathers, if you obey the voice of

the Lord your God to keep His commandments and His statutes which are written in this book of the Law ... (vv. 9-10)

This is the outcome, the soul-deep experience of being favored by God—"a special possession"! Gone is the victim consciousness, the slave-mentality, the sense of being a non-entity, an outcast, a wanderer, exile, or a faceless, nameless number on the fringes of life.

... and if you turn to the Lord your God with all your heart and with all your soul. (v. 10)

But it requires strength, discipline, focus, and an unwavering preference for an authentic relationship with the Highest Energy, the Creative Powers of Love and Life.

A MESSAGE TO ME:

Use your journal to write, draw, or expand upon your own impressions.

The Source and the Choice

The remaining nine verses of this great chapter of Deuteronomy 30 state with absolute certainty where this compassionate and powerful Creative Source is found and point to the undodgeable responsibility of personal choice. In the readings, Edgar Cayce quoted these remaining verses more often than any other part of the Old Testament. As the most frequently quoted and recommended Old Testament verse in the Edgar Cayce readings, Moses' discourse in Deuteronomy 30 shares a vital relationship with John 14-17, the most frequently quoted and recommended New Testament verse. Both passages represent the last discourse and final teachings in the earthly ministry of these great teachers.

In his Bible study recommendations, Cayce often suggested Deuteronomy and the Book of John be studied together. Of this highly recommended Old Testament chapter, two verses are the most often quoted and amplified: the verses on the Source and the Choice. Apparently, Moses' conclusions on the location of Source (vv. 11-14) and the power of our Choices (vv. 15-19) were considered worthy of our deepest meditation.

IT IS NOT TOO HARD FOR YOU
THE SOURCE

For this commandment which I command you today is not too mysterious for you, nor is it far off. It is not in heaven, that you should say, "Who will bring it to us, that we may hear it and do it?" Nor is it beyond the sea, that you should say, "Who will bring it to us, that we may hear it and do it?" But the word is very near you, in your mouth and in your heart, that you may do it. (vv. 11-12)

THE WISDOM OF THE EDGAR CAYCE READINGS

. . . much must be taken into consideration that would be only understood by those who have turned within and who know themselves as being souls, and as bearing direct relationships to Creative Forces. Those may not understand who only see the material or mental world, and who know little of spirit or of soul and as to its activity. For, indeed it is true that ye must seek if ye would find. As given of old, and as ye may read, it is not who shall descend from heaven to give thee a message, nor who should come from over the sea; for Lo, it is within thine own self. 294-198 This, then, is all-inclusive, yet may be better discerned in the study and the application of the tenets set in the thirtieth (30th) of Deuteronomy by the lawgiver in his admonition, in his summing up of the laws, the ordinances that had been indicated for a peculiar people, set aside for a purpose—as a channel through which there might be the discerning of the spirit made manifest in flesh. 2879-1 When self can look the world and all straight in the face, and move on towards the better things, forgetting that which is behind, moving on to the higher forces that will be the creating of the faith, confidence, and of the purposes that will be set before thee from day to day, then the inner man will find peace, harmony, happiness, joy in service; for he that is the greatest among you is the servant of all! 1264-1 For, as was given of old—Say not as to who will descend from heaven that ye may have a message, for Lo, it is in thine own heart. For, thy body is indeed the temple of the living God. There He—as all knowledge, all undertakings, all wisdom, all understanding—may commune with thee, if ye but give that opportunity, that force an opportunity to open thine heart, thine mind, thy understanding, to His presence . . . How do ye open? By attuning, turning thy thought, thy purpose, thy desire to be at an at-onement with Him. The atonement has been offered. Thus ye have that assurance that as ye seek His face He will come and abide. 2533-4 For we all—and ye are as others—are gods in the making: not the God, but gods in the making! For He would have thee be one with Him. Then when ye reason from these activities in thy daily associations ye find it becomes as was given of old, not as a formula or ritual, or that ye should cry "Who shall go over the earth and bring a message, or who shall descend from heaven or arise from hell that I may know—for Lo, He is with thee!" 877-21

Moses is one of the great leaders in history. To those he led, it must have seemed as if he had a special relationship with God, one that they lacked. And, on occasion, such as at Meribah (Numbers 20:10-11) Moses seemed to confirm that perception—creating a division between him, the spiritually annointed, divinely chosen leader, and them, the balking, complaining, defective, and dysfunctional followers.

However, the greatness in Moses' leadership was founded on the fact that he was a seeker and a meditator. By continually seeking guidance from the Source in meditation through the years, Moses' consciousness and abilities expanded greatly. In the beginning, he was fearful and doubtful of his abilities. The Voice that spoke to him at the Burning Bush entrusted him to deliver the messages to pharaoh, but Moses balked, saying he was a stutterer and slow of speech. Who would listen to him!

Every character in the Bible demonstrates some form of weakness and failing as a full and complete manifestation of the Divine Image and the Christ Consciousness—except one. " . . . even in Elijah or John we find the faltering, the doubting," Cayce said. "We find no faltering, no doubting, no putting aside of the purpose in the Master Jesus." (3054-4)

As the emotonally volatile Egyptian prince, Moses "slew a man in his wrath." His temper flares again on Mt. Sinai when he shatters the tablets of stone. Edgar Cayce, in his Bible class, notes with good humor and insight into human nature, that while Moses was always ready to excoriate the people for their backsliding, he never acknowledges or admits that his throwing down the tablets of stone in a fit of rage is a shortcoming of his. Throughout the wilderness journey, he had been the great leader. People hung on his every word. They came to him seeking advice and guidance. He was the last word on all issues great and small. Who wouldn't have an ego problem!

Yet at Mt. Nebo, where Deuteronomy is shared in his

last days, Moses speaks from the depth of his experience after "he had finished all of his own egotism." (262-100) He is a man of peace who submits totally to the will of the Divine. He accepts that he will not be allowed to enter the Promised Land. By stepping back and anointing a new leader, Joshua, he fulfills his purpose and completes his mission. His life mission was to lead the Israelites out of bondage; his soul challenge was to transform the ego and spiritualize his anger.

The capacity for spiritual leadership and authority resides in everybody, even in the complaining, stiff-necked, rebellious generation Moses led through the wilderness. Even in the complaining, rebellious, difficult people we encounter today. We all have the capacity for a unique and personal relationship with God. We are all souls, spiritual beings endowed with imperishable birthrights. We have the capability to subdue the earth and multiply blessings: "The word is very near—on our lips and in our hearts, so we may do it."

A MESSAGE TO ME:

Use your journal to write, draw, or expand upon your own impressions.

CHOOSE THOU

THE CHOICE
Deuteronomy 30:15-16,19-20

See, I have set before you life and good, death and evil, in that I command you today to love the Lord your God, to walk in His ways, and to keep His commandments, His statutes, His judg-

ments, that you may live and multiply . . .

I call heaven and earth as witnesses today against you, that I have set before you life and death, blessing and cursing; therefore choose life, that both you and your descendants may live; that you may love the Lord your God, that you may obey His voice, and that you may cling to Him, for He is your life and the length of your days; and that you may dwell in the land which the Lord swore to your fathers, to Abraham, Isaac, and Jacob, to give them.

THE WISDOM OF THE EDGAR CAYCE READINGS

Whatever thy choice is, let these be ever with an eye single to service to that living influence of being a better, a greater channel of blessings to someone. Not of self choosing an easier way; not of self attempting to escape that as is necessary for thine own understanding, thine own soul development, but rather ever, "Thy will, O Lord, be done in and through me—Use me as Thou seest I have need of, that I may be a *living* example of Thy love, of Thy guidance in this material experience." 845-4 Then cultivate—in thy mind, in thy body—those attributes which are endowed with that seeking for the knowledge of the true relationship of every soul with its Maker . . . And it is according to thy own choice as to whether these are constantly constructive, creative, or for the satisfying of material appetites. For know, it is ever as He hath given—Today, *now,* there is set before thee good and evil, life and death—Choose thou! 1754-1

It is difficult indeed to overstate the emphasis and importance of personal choice in our destiny. It is a prominent theme throughout the Bible and in the Cayce readings, and underscored and highlighted in the recommended Bible study verses.

After he breathes the first breath of life, Adam's next awareness is that he must make choices. The principle of choice is stated and restated in every promise and prophecy in the Bible. All the promises are conditional. There is a cause-and-effect result to every action, every choice. "If you will be my people, I will be your God." Moses understood that very well and impressed its significance on all the generations that followed him.

Moses came to his conclusions about the Source and the Choice through his experience in the wilderness. There is little that the world can teach you in the wilderness, for it is not a place where the worldly live. In the wilderness, we are no longer who we used to be and not yet what we are to become. Here we must learn to trust our intuition, to rely upon our inner voice, and to find strength and support in a principle that is in this world, but not of it. The wilderness period is always characterized by the struggle within ourselves as we seek to surrender to the highest part of ourselves, the universal mind, the cosmic self—trust it, act on it, be transformed by it, and ultimately—to become it.

EXERCISE: CHOICE

When you consider both the "blessings" and the "curses" in your life, can you connect them to patterns of choice that you have made?

CHOICES AND OUTCOMES TO CONSIDER

To have more happiness in your life—what must you choose?

To have greater health in your life—what choices do you have to make soon?

To have more fulfilling relationships—what do you

have to do that you are not doing now?

To achieve greater satisfaction in your work or career—what is the most important choice you can make now?

One definition of insanity is continuing to make the same choices and expecting a different result. Do you agree?

David Consciousness

Introduction to the Psalms

In the Scripture, David is more than the name of a historical figure, but it also signifies a spiritual condition or inner awareness. According to the Edgar Cayce source, the name David vibrates at a very high spiritual frequency. The designation *David* indicates:

> ... [a] gift from the higher forces, or a son of the Father [and] one, especially, endowed with gifts from the higher forces. 137-13

The name David can be used as a power point to

achieve a feeling of self-affirmation within and, perhaps, confidence concerning gifts and talents and the ability to express and accomplish spiritual purposes in a material world.

As Divine Images, we all have the potential and ability to be "a gift of the Higher Forces." And, we can be assured we are all "endowed with gifts" from that same Source.

Consider the synergy of the power points we have covered so far:

• The Genesis birthrights of Light, Divine Self-Awareness, and Mastery

• The four principles of Eden awareness

• The power to turn "evil tempter" into spiritual guide

• The evolutionary potential of Exodus 19:5, the Ten Commandments, and the Seven Challenges of Moses

• The location of the Source and the power of Choice in Deuteronomy 30

As a foundation of archetypal patterns, these power points, individually and as a system, possess an energy that can carry us to the inescapable realization that we, also, are "a gift of the Higher Forces," and exceptionally fortified with a multitude of gifts, talents, and abilities waiting to be experienced, explored, and expressed. After all, as Nelson Mandela expressed in his 1994 inaugural speech, who are we not to be brilliant, gorgeous, talented, and fabulous?

"Be fruitful and multiply" isn't a suggestion, it's a command! We just have to expand our awareness to the place within us where we know that to be absolutely true.

Rememberest thou all that has been given as to the manner in which the individual finds self? Did Moses receive direction save by the period in the

Mount? Did Samuel receive rather than by the meditating within his own closet? Did David not find more within the meditating within the valley and the cave? 707-6

MEDITATION EXERCISE: DAVID CONSCIOUSNESS

Take a few breaths to clear the mind and relax the body. Each breath is a gift, a gift of life. Begin this meditation by focusing on your appreciation for this gift of life and for the opportunities you have for expressing who you are.

Take a moment to recall a time when you received a gift that you truly loved and enjoyed. Relive the feelings of that exerience fully and completely now.

Now, with a sense of gratitude and appreciation, bring to mind a person in your life—a parent, relative, teacher, friend, lover, mate, child—whose presence at a particular time in your life was like a gift to you. And reexperience fully and completely that feeling of gratitude and appreciation for that person.

Now take a moment and allow your deeper mind to bring into your awareness a person from another time in your life who felt this way toward you—that your presence was a gift to him or her, as friend, counselor, parent, child, teacher, co-worker. And allow that person's feelings of love and appreciation to be experienced by you now.

Now dismiss those images and, with your next breath, go deeper and deeper yet into this feeling of gifts and gratitude and love. Be aware of the many gifts you have been told you have, special talents and abilities people recognize and appreciate in you—gifts you've had from birth or that you developed in school. A talent for sports or math, music or art. A gift of gab, of socializing. Gifts that have always been a part of you. And others that have unfolded in the course of your life—abilities emerging out of life's challenges and demands; gifts of endurance, persistence, patience; gifts of insight and understanding, of planning, of organization or spontaneity; gifts of relationship skills; even gifts born through loss and disappointment. Gifts that have come early, abilities that have come late.

Emmerse yourself in the consciousness of these gifts. Now allow that part of your mind that is the Divine Mind to speak to that part of your Mind that is the human mind. Listen, accept, and be aware totally, fully, and completely without hesitation or reservaton that what you have, what you are is *a gift from the higher forces. You are a Son, a Daughter of the Father/Mother/Everything God.*

And when you reach that level of mind, where the Deeper Mind—that consciousness within you that has knowledge of God and is present with the Divine—is one with the human mind that has knowledge and beliefs about who you are and what you aren't, take another breath and know, at this level of the mind, you are one with David—David consciousness. Know now *totally and compeletly, without resisting or negating in any way—you are especially endowed with gifts from the Higher Forces,* gifts perhaps that are not yet fully unwrapped or even discovered.

Now take one of these gifts and unwrap it. See the gift unfolding in your life. How does it change or improve your life? What is the effect it has on others?

Now let the image go, and know that if David is a power point word for you, you can use it anytime to connect with your gifts and to your source. If not, know there are other names you can use equally as well whenever you need to know life is a gift and that you have all the abilities, skills, and talents that you need to bring a multitude of gifts into this world.

A GIFT OF THE HIGHER FORCES

The twelve tribes of Israel have their roots in an astrological model. They represent the twelve signs of the zodiac, which in turn represent twelve primary energy patterns. In the language of the readings, the twelve astrological signs represents the twelve manners of expression, the twelve dimensions of consciousness in this solar system. The four elements, like the twelve astrological forces, are meant to be allies supporting the growth, development, unfolding, and spiritualization of the ego in the earth.

While Abraham received the promise, and Jacob fathered twelve sons, and Moses led the twelve tribes for forty years, and Joshua, as their leader, brought the twelve tribes into the land of the promise, David was the first king to unify the twelve tribes of Israel and to establish a "sacred center"—the city of Jerusalem.

In the ancient view, the world was thought to radiate from a divine center. Anchored by a secure power point, the "world"—defined as the sphere of influence under the control of a particular ruler or deity—was symbolically divided into four equal quarters, or sections, with lines radiating out from the center to the four cardinal points of the compass and inscribed with a circle. Inside the sacred circle, the ruler of the realm, whether human or god, sat at the center point, and from this sacred center, order and harmony emanated to the four corners of the world. Outside of the circle, chaos, darkness, infidels, monsters, and evil forces prevailed.

Those familiar with the concept of mandalas will recognize the image of a quadrated circle with an organizing center as a mandala. Psychologically, the ruler represents the ego, or self, and the realm—represented by a circle with a center and divided into four equal sections—is a representation of "psychological and spiritual" wholeness.

At the height of his reign, David sat at the "spiritual center" of the world, with lines of power emanating to the ends of the earth. As the "organizing power" in the center of the circle, David is, symbolically speaking, the first "whole person" in the Bible.

In the ancient world, and in many tribal cultures, the only "whole" person was the ruler. All other tribal members were defined and specialized into roles or functions. They were either warriors, shamans, hunters, or farmers. Only the tribal leader or chief as ruler, warrior, magician/shaman, and lover embodied all of the major roles or functions in one person. In other words, in order to "sit in the center" all sides of the psyche had to be developed. (*King, Warrior, Magician, Lover*, Robert Moore and Douglas Gillette, HarperSan Francisco, 1990)

Through the birthright of "Dominion" (Genesis 1:27), we are designed to be rulers. We are designed to be sovereign in our own domain, or sphere of influence. As "sovereign rulers" in our own domain, we need to govern our "sacred center" and allow its power and intelligence to flow out to all four directions of the soul—body, mind, spirit, and emotions—and to infuse them all with power.

Robert Moore and Douglas Gillette suggest in their book by the same name that *King, Warrior, Magician, Lover* are four major archetypes that, when expressed positively, define the nature of mature masculine energy. By substituting Ruler for King, these same four archetypes, or primary energy patterns, may also be equally relevant in the definition of mature feminine energy.

Regardless, the purpose of this exercise is to work with

the concept of the four archetypes, the sacred circle, and the associations with David (as a spiritual power point) to create your own experience with "wholeness" through your "gifts from Higher Power."

To do this, first we have to recognize the functions of the four archetypes and how we relate to them.

RULER:

David was ruler of his domain.

The ruler is sovereign in his or her domain, or sphere of influence. When the ruler archetype is active in our lives and expressing positively, we feel at home in the physical world and in charge of ourselves. We enjoy life and are comfortable in the process of expressing who we are and have some confidence that we know how to get our needs met.

Carol Pearson in *Awakening the Heroes Within* notes that in the old legends and fairy tales, the royal child is often raised unaware of his or her royal blood. Only after confronting many obstacles and challenges does it become clear to the hero or heroine that he or she is the long lost child of a great and royal house, and destined to rule. This is a parable, too, of our own process of coming to power. David was the youngest of his brothers and the least likely, in terms of family dynamics and traditions of the times, to be cast in a leadership position. However as a shepherd, he learned how to care for his flock and to fend off wolves and bears—experiences that prepared him for his rise in stature and power.

Every challenge we face, every fear we overcome is an opportunity to be that much closer to having our divinity revealed!

WARRIOR:

David was victorious in many battles "in service" to the Divine.

When the warrior energy is expressing positively in our lives, it provides us with the capacity to take appropriate action when the boundaries of our physical, psychological, or spiritual domain are threatened. Without a strong warrior we have no defense against the demands and intrusions of others. The most positive aspect of the Warrior is illustrated in David's relationship to Saul, when Saul sought his life. Even though his rise to power had turned Saul into a negative ruler, David honored the fact that Saul was anointed by the prophet Samuel and never harmed him, even though Saul plotted continually against him. David outwitted Saul as a strategist and even though he had many opportunities to seize power and slay Saul, he never used his power against him.

The aggressive nature of the warrior is never on behalf of self, but in service to the Ruler, or a higher principle. The Warrior's aggressiveness is expressed in an attitude toward life that rouses energies and motivates one to take action. The Warrior energy allows us to leap into the fray full of vital energy, rather than simply maintaining a defensive or holding position about life's tasks and challenges.

MAGICIAN:

David's psalms are one of the legacies of his "magic."

A Magician knows how to manipulate energy and create change. David demonstrates his skill as a magician when, with only harp and song, he relieves King Saul of the demons that trouble his soul. Every time we experience the beautiful, calming, centering effect of the Twenty-third Psalm, we are experiencing David's magic again.

Accessing our magician allows us to channel and direct our power. When a mother soothes her child's boo-boo's with a healing touch and a gentle word, she is expressing magician energy. Remember the promise of Exodus 1:5—if we heed the Voice, we shall become a nation of valued beings—priests and "special treasures."

The Magician is another aspect of the priest and shaman—a bridge between seen and unseen worlds. A Magician has knowledge of things hidden or not easily seen or understood by the practical, rational, and pragmatically minded. A Magician's awareness tends toward inner processes, hidden dynamics, and things concealed. According to Moore and Gillette, the Magician is also associated with the "Observing Ego," that part of ourselves that can step outside of ourselves and watch us walk by.

Because of their wisdom and deep thought, their capacity to see clearly, and their knowledge of secret wisdom, Magicians were invaluable allies in preserving the integrity of the realm. David was fluid and could make instant change. When his "sins" were brought to his attention by his spiritual advisor, Nathan, David was quick to make adjustments and restore connection to his spiritual center.

In addition to keeping prophets and spiritual advisors around him, David often went into the caves and mountains to meditate—to access the deeper wisdom and knowing at the center of the soul. He was a true Magician.

LOVER:

There are many and varied ways that King David expresses the energy of the Lover.

We need only recall the famous story of David's love

for Bathsheba to identify him with the Lover energy. But David's soul also "knit" with Jonathan, Saul's son, and their story of friendship is legendary.

The Lover energy in us wants to reach out, touch, connect with life, and express the fullness of our feelings and emotion as they are experienced within. According to Moore and Gillette, the Lover is felt in the healthy embodiment of being in one's body without shame, of experiencing connection to the world and the people around us. When David brought the Ark of the Covenant into Jerusalem, he danced exuberantly in the streets clad only in a loin cloth, to the scorn of his wife, Abigail, whose heart turned cold against him.

On another level, the Lover energy sweeps us into mystical communion with all things—with nature, with the Divine, with our fellow beings. Lover delights through words of authentic praise and concrete actions that enhance the lives of others.

Lovers are not necessarily concerned with keeping order, setting laws, or following rules as is the King, or maintaining discipline and keeping alert and focused as

ACCESSING THE IMAGE

is the Warrior, or even of mastering the mysteries of the Magician. The Lover wants to love and live intensely, feeling and celebrating his or her deep connection with life. David's whole, deep, rich, intense life expresses the energy of the Lover.

THE SACRED CENTER

Take a moment to close your eyes and meditate briefly on each of the quadrants. As you focus on each section, allow your own feelings to come up in relation to the archetype.

How "good" is your Ruler?

How "strong" is your Warrior?

How "skillful" is your Magician?

How "connected and passionate" is your Lover?

Describe a time in your life when you were in touch with these archetypes?

Which are strongest in your life? Which feel undeveloped?

What would you look and act like if all four of these archetypes were functioning harmoniously in a positive manner?

In the appropriate quadrant, write in the positive qualities you feel you currently possess that relate to each of the four archetypes. Place any negatives outside the circle near the appropriate section. Use the chart on p. 190 as a reference.

IN THE CENTER OF THE WORLD

You can do the following exercise as a guided meditation experience or acted out with bodily movement. For maximum effect and to facilitate neurological change, it should engage the whole body.

If these terms fit, put them in the circle in the appropriate space. Add your own definitions if you don't find them here.

QUALITIES

POSITIVE	NEGATIVE
KING	
Organizes, maintains control	Dogmatic
Self-expression	Rigid
Sees and brings out best in others	Inflexible
	Aloof
	Control Freak
WARRIOR	
Courageous	Overly aggressive
Decisive	No emotions, cold, calculating
Code of honor	Reaching the goal is everything, no matter what it takes or who gets hurt
Clear thinking	
Sticks with goals	
Keeps commitments	Confrontational over every issue
Lives by principles	Must prove himself superior at all costs
Fights for what matters	
	Masks feelings of powerlessness with aggressiveness
MAGICIAN	
Inner wisdom	Uses powers to control others
Trusts intuition	Diffused, unfocused thinking
Knowledge of hidden things, deep truths, interpersonal dynamics	Takes advantage of others by manipulating emotions or mind control
Performs "miracles"	Egotism
Can change consciousness at will	
Mastery over the tools of his or her trade or profession	
LOVER	
Engages with life	Afraid to feel
Connection to others	Head rules heart
Exudes charisma	Lusting
Expresses passion that unites body, heart, and soul	Jealous
Compassionate	Tendency toward rage or icy feelings
Empathetic	
Caring	
Loses self in mystical oneness	

Imagine you are standing in the center of a circle, and this circle represents your world, the realm over which you have influence and power.

Notice how large your circle is. Can you make your circle even larger?

Now, as you stand in the center of your circle, imagine four lines radiating out from the center to the edge of your circle, dividing the circle into four equal sections.

Take a moment now to connect to this center of power and allow your mind, or your imagination, to connect to the energy of all those who have stood in their center of power. Be aware of the images, names, or scenes that come into your awareness.

Now, without being concerned about the actual direction you are facing, imagine you are aligned with the direction of north. A line radiates from you to the edge of the circle, and at the edge of the circle, in the direction of north, stands a powerful Ruler, a king or queen, perhaps a mighty tribal chieftain. And as you face this Ruler, you are aware of the line that radiates from this sacred center and connects you to him or her. And through the line, power and energy are flowing to you and from you. This line of power has a specific color, too, and perhaps you can hear the sound of the energy flowing.

The Ruler is here to give you power and authority to be the ruler of your own domain and to help you prosper. This line represents your connection to him or her. Walk now in the path of the power toward the Ruler and, as you approach him or her, feel his or her energy and confidence. The Ruler has a gift for you. Now take another step and step into the Ruler and merge with this energy. Feel it totally and completely. Now turn and face the center, and see yourself standing there, without this gift, and know why it was given to you. Now dissolve the image and return to the center.

Now turn to the right until you face the direction of east. A line goes out from where you stand to the edge of the circle, and at the edge of the circle, in the direction of east, stands a powerful Warrior, an ancient knight, a samurai, or perhaps a Native American warrior or Amazon queen.

This Warrior is your ally; and as you face him or her, you are suddenly aware that a line of power connects you to him or her; and you can feel power and energy flowing to you. This Warrior energy has a specific color, too, and perhaps you can hear the sound of the energy flowing.

The Warrior is here to give you what it already possesses—the courage and power and decisiveness to fight the only enemies that matter—the enemies that lie within. Walk toward the Warrior now, and as you approach him or her, be aware of what the Warrior gives you. Your mind is clear, your steps are sure and firm. Feel the energy as you draw closer.

When you reach the Warrior, merge with the energy until it becomes your own. Now turn and face the center and see yourself as you were before this gift was given. Dissolve the image and walk on the line of power back to the center of your circle.

And now, turn again until you are aligned with the third line of power in the direction of south. A line radiates from you to the edge of the circle, and at the edge of the circle, in the direction of south stands a being who embodies all the energies of the Lover, perhaps a poet, an artist, a pioneer, an adventurer, or mystical radiant being. As you face the Lover, you are aware of the line that radiates from where you stand at your sacred center and connects you to him or her. And through the line, power and energy are flowing. This line of power has its own color, too, and perhaps you can hear the sound of the energy flowing as you face the Lover.

The Lover is not constrained or restrained by his or her own deep emotions and powerful feelings. The Lover lives its passion fully and completely and celebrates its connection to all that it loves. The Lover beckons to you to come forward, to step into its energy, to open your heart and feel the adventure and the joy, the sadness and the sorrows of living and to celebrate it all.

And as you walk toward the Lover, you merge its energy with your whole body, mind, and spirit. You feel it totally and completely throughout your whole being. The Lover's power envelops you in a feeling that is enjoyable, sensuous, and spiritual. And when you feel ready, turn and face the center of the circle. See yourself as you were, without the Lover's energy, and dissolve the image. In its place now, there you are as the Ruler facing north, as Warrior looking east; and now as you walk back to the center, you add the energy of the Lover to the center.

And now, turn again to the right until you are aligned with the fourth and final line of power in the direction of west. A line radiates from you to the edge of the circle, and at the edge of the circle, in the direction of west stands a wise and powerful Magician, sage, priest, shaman, or priestess. As you face the Magician, you are aware of the line that radiates from this sacred center and connects you to him or her. This line of power has a specific color, too, and you can hear the sound of the energy flowing.

The Magician is here to initiate you, to make you aware of your power, your natural ability to change and grow and to extend beyond the limits of your body, the limits of your senses, to help you understand the mysteries and how to use them wisely. Walk down that line of power toward the Magician and, as you do, feel his or her energy. Open your soul and listen with your spirit to what secrets the Magician communicates to you. Feel the energy of knowing and wisdom. Step closer, until you and the Magician merge and become one—his greatest magic. When you feel ready, turn and face the circle. See yourself as you were before, without this power and wisdom, and dissolve the image.

In its place, the Ruler is facing north, the Warrior looks to the east, the Lover stands gazing south. All of them are you, and now you as Magician walk back on the line of power to the center and stand with your other selves.

Take a deep breath now and float up above the circle; and you are looking down at the four lines of power radiating out from the center to the edge of the circle, forming four equal sections. The Ruler, Warrior, Lover, and Magician stand in their places at the edge of the circle, looking in, with lines of power connecting you to them. Realize now these are your allies, and they are a part of you, ready to give you guidance, strength, ability, passion to fulfill your purpose with power equal to David's— and even greater. Now with your next breath, float down to the center of the circle and breathe in the power of each energy, and know that at any time you choose, you can return to this center or call on any of the powers.

For a complete story about David from the Edgar Cayce point of view, see Volume 2, *Edgar Cayce's Story of the Old Testament,* A.R.E. Press, chapters 6 & 7, pp. 112-180.

A Book of Psalms

Read the 1st of the Psalms, the 24th, the 91st, the 23rd and the 150th; and you will find them . . . as the expression of the experience of an individual entity, a soul—as self—seeking to know the greater, the better, the more helpful relationships to Creative Forces. 1317-1

A SUGGESTED APPROACH TO THE PSALMS

The psalms most frequently recommended as power points by Edgar Cayce are Psalms 1, 23, 24, 91, and 150. A sixth psalm, Psalm 8, is also included.

Like almost all the psalms of the Old Testament, the six psalms included for study here are actually little treatises on meditation as related to a "peak awareness." While not all the psalms were written by David, his name is synonymous with them. In the Bible, David is a soul who is fully engaged in life. He is warrior, statesman, poet, king, father, lover, musician, visionary, architect, city planner, and nation builder.

Though not perfect and beset with human weakness, David consistently sought to align himself with his spiritual center and to act from that consciousness. Whenever he erred, Nathan, his spiritual counselor and alter ego, rebuked him with unvarnished truth. As warrior and king and lover, David was quick to accept the corrections, make amends, and realign to the Divine Within.

> Study as to why David is called "a man—man—after God's own heart." Not that he was free from fault, but that his purposes, his hopes, his fears were continually submitted to God. 4047-2

David lived the ideal expressed in Exodus 19:5: He listened to the voice, followed its leadings, and became a special possession and a treasure. But this promise is true for all of us as well.

It has been said that the Bible is God's word to us, but the Psalms are our word to God. Through the ages, the Psalms have lent themselves to freer, more personal forms of interpretation than most other portions of the Scripture. This is due, in part, to their poetry but even more to the fact that they are expressions of spiritual emotions aroused by the facts of human existence. These songs express the heights of human experience, and their chords strike resonance in the soul.

These six psalms may not all have actually originated with David, but they fit under the canopy of *David Consciousness.*

"MAKE IT AN EXPERIENCE OF SELF"

All of the psalms were meant to be sung and accompanied by music—or at least, spoken out loud.

To begin:

- Read each psalm slowly and silently to yourself. Spend a few minutes meditating upon the messages you discover in them. Note which images, words, or thoughts have the most emotional tone for you.
- Next, read one psalm out loud, slowly.
- Read it out loud again. This time explore different intonations, tone modulation, and vocal emphasis with your voice. Note how the meanings change as you explore with the tones and values of sound, silently or out loud, focusing not on the meaning of the words, but on the feelings which the poem expresses. Read it several more times, not as a dramatic reading, but exploring the right emotional tone and expression that fit the feeling of the poem as you understand it. Allow yourself to become more creative and experimental with your approach.

In his multifaceted, multidimensional life, David lived and played out many roles. He was a warrior, ruler, lover, philospher, sage, and magician. All of these roles David played as he composed, meditated upon, and chanted the psalms. Which voice suits the psalm best? Which voice suits you best?

As you read the psalms out loud, sound them in the voice of these different roles—in the voice of one who is the confident ruler of the realm. Sound it in the voice of a spiritual warrior, of a lover, a poet, and a magician.

Now close your eyes. What image or images from the poem come to mind? What feelings, insights, impressions come into your awareness with each voice?

- When you feel ready, write or draw them out in your journal.
- If you are in a study group, read the psalm together out loud, and discuss your feelings.

- Discuss various ideas concerning the psalms. And remember, nobody is right or wrong, simply allow a sharing of ideas and responses.

MAKING FRIENDS WITH THE PSALMS

When you receive a "gift" from the psalm, know you have made a "friend" of it. With your eyes closed, take a few moments to relax and then begin meditating on one of the psalms which has given you a "gift."

Be aware of the images and feelings which are strongest for you. And use those feelings to imagine what state of mind, what feelings moved the author to write these words. Allow your mind to create an imagined scene, or event, which is the inspiration for the psalm. Trust your imagination and allow the feelings and images to come up without any real effort or forcing on your part. What experience caused it to be written down? Who was it that was so uplifted, so inspired, so confident, or so in need of contact with Spiritual Forces to have that experience? What happened? Where were they? Trust your imagination, and let the visualization follow its own energy.

Allow your imagination to take you in any direction it chooses. Don't be concerned if what you experience or see isn't an angel, biblical character or setting. Simply be aware of how your unconscious mind responds to the suggestions.

When you have a sense of a presence or spiritual guide connected to the psalm, ask for a name and more information, if you wish. Ask for help to understand the psalm spiritually or for other insights that the psalm or the guide can give you.

This can be a very powerful experience. Even if you choose not to do this type of guided visualization, know that to meditate and muse upon these sacred songs with curiosity and a desire to experience "truth" will bring a "guide" or teacher close to you.

Using the psalm as a power point of communication and inspiration is an ancient way of establishing contact with your spiritual guides (and you have many) as well as contacting the guardians of the archetypes of spiritual Israel.

Like a Tree

Blessed is the man who walks not in the counsel of the
wicked,
nor stands in the way of sinners,
nor sits in the seat of scoffers,
but his delight is in the law of the Lord,
and on his law he meditates day and night.

He is like a tree planted by the streams of water,
that yields its fruit in its season,
and its leaf does not wither.
In all that he does he prospers.

The wicked are not so, but are like chaff
which the wind drives away.
Therefore the wicked will not stand in judgment,
nor sinner in the congregation of the righteous;
for the Lord knows the way of the righteous,
but the way of the wicked shall perish.

THE WISDOM OF THE EDGAR CAYCE READINGS

Read more oft the law of love . . . Grow in spiritual understanding, that thy mental and thy physical manifestations
in thy relationships to others, and conditions, may be tem-
pered with that mercy, that justice, that kindness, that
patience, as ye would have thy Lord, thy God, thy Savior,
have with thee . . . Hence that injunction . . . Delight in the
law of the Lord; meditate on same day and night; and
then all phases of thy experience ye will be happy, harmonious, *and* successful in every phase of thy relationships .
. . Thus ye will find that thy will, thy temperament, will
become more and more able to be gentle, patient, kind,
long-suffering, with brotherly love; and these are indeed
the fruits of the spirit. And they that manifest such in their
daily life walk close with Him in every way. 2062-1

Quotations and allusions from psalm 1 are sparse in
the Edgar Cayce readings, yet this keynote psalm is
among the most consistently recommended psalms for
study. Undoubtedly, the emphasis on meditation offers
a clue to its importance.

Bible scholars regard "the law of the Lord" referred to
in this psalm as a reference to the codified and written
law. The Edgar Cayce readings, as in other mystical traditions, acknowledge the law in its spiritual sense, as inner guidance and instruction of God. Indeed, this is
implied in the original meaning of Torah as Law and, no
doubt, is the source of joy discovered by the author of
this wonderfully concise wisdom song.

Through meditation, we make contact with the Light
Within and begin to experience the Divine Image. *"Delight in the law of the Lord; meditate on same day and
night,"* Cayce told the support group that formed around
him seeking advice and guidance on spiritual growth,

"and . . . ye will be happy, harmonious, and successful in every phase of thy relationships."
With the mind centered in the Light, we can more clearly discern the insights, intuition, and revelations of the still small voice of the deeper Mind. Through meditation, we can control what happens in our minds and bodies—we gain "dominion" over the reactiveness of our natural defenses and unconscious, painful memories.

Take a few moments and reflect on one or more of the laws we have observed so far in this study:

Let there be Light.

Be fruitful and multiply.

If you eat from the tree, ye shall surely die.

If you obey my voice and heed my command . . . you shall become a special treasure.

Ask not who shall ascend the mountain . . . the message is within you.

There is set before you life and death, choose! . . . you create the results you must live with.

QUESTIONS FOR REFLECTION

Which day of the week are you most likely to meditate or reflect upon your purpose in life, and how do the events, relationships, and circumstances of your life reflect the perfect working out of personal lessons, challenges, and opportunities for spiritual growth?

Are you most likely to have these meditations in the morning, afternoon, or evening?

When you consider the laws of karma, of cause and effect, do they inspire you with awe and respect for Divine Love?

Do you find reason to celebrate that you are responsible for your choices?

How often do you release judgment and accept that everything is operating according to a divine plan, or according to spiritual laws?

The readings indicate that to see imperfection in the world is to minimize the consciousness of God's power and perfection. Is this a challenging idea for you?

If the Laws of the Lord are perfect, how do you explain or relate to the fact of suffering, sorrow, injustice, inequality, famine, warfare, violence in the world—and can you find "delight" in your answer?

TREE OF LIFE

He shall be like a tree
that yields its fruit in its season,
and its leaf does not wither. (Ps.1:3)

THE WISDOM OF THE EDGAR CAYCE READINGS

Build not a one-sided life, know that he that is well-grounded is as a tree planted by the waters of life, that given out is as for the healings of many—whether in those of the mental forces or those of the material gains of life; and let not thine physical endeavors be evil-spoken of. 1727-1

How easily, then, must it have been said, that it hath not yet entered into the mind of man as to the unspeakable glories of him who has washed his raiment in the blood of the Lamb, who has made himself one in thought, in deed, in body, one with that through that purpose, that mind of God . . . For when those activities become such that the Mind of the individual, of the soul, finds itself expressing itself in the physical, in the mental, the body will take on what? Immortality! In the earth? Yes; reflecting same that it may bring what is as the tree of life in the garden, that its leaves are for the healings of the nations; that are the leaves that may fall from thy lips, from thy activities to thy fellow man, in whatever sphere or realm of activity. Why? Because of thine own self, because thou art grounded in the water of life itself, as ye grow upon those inflowings and outflowings of the spirit of Him that gave, "Let that mind be in you which is in me, that as I abide in the Father and ye abide in me, we may be one with Him," which is the destiny of those that love His coming. 262-78

To "delight in the laws of the Lord" brings a natural consequence. The joyful meditator becomes a Tree.

The Tree is a multidimensional archetype. It is both a metaphor for a person well rooted in spiritual laws and in harmony with his or her divine nature, and, in this psalm, is also a reference back to the kabbalistic Tree of Life we encountered in the Seven Challenges of Moses at the bitter pool and in the victory over the Amalekites. This Tree is the same one that grows in the center of the Garden of Eden.

The importance of this Tree is highlighted and underscored in the Scripture through the places where we find it. It occurs in Eden with the appearance of Adam. It reappears in Psalm 1 as a keynote chord for the rest of the Psalter. And the Tree makes its final appearance in the last chapter of the New Testament, to seal the book. It is present at the beginning and the end and woven throughout.

We have seen veiled references to it in the Seven Challenges of Moses, and it is prominent in several passages recommended in the Edgar Cayce Bible study recommendations. The Tree of Life is encountered in Genesis 1 and Psalm 1. Jeremiah prophesies about the Tree of Life (17:8) and the prophet Daniel tells the startled Nebuchadnezzar that the great and overshadowing tree that is chopped down at the root in his famous dream, "O king, is you." (Daniel 4)

Jesus in John 15 speaks of himself as "a vine" and we as the branches, a variation on the Tree image. The cross of Jesus is often referred to as the Tree of Life. And on the hill of Golgotha, with Jesus in the middle and the two thieves on either side, we again see the reflection of the kabbalistic Tree of Life, with Jesus as the middle path and the "good" and the "bad" reflecting the pillars of mercy and severity.

As the Tree of Life, the Cross is central to the mystery of the Resurrection and the path toward immortality— for without the resurrection, the ministry and miracles of Jesus would count for little more than a footnote in history, as Cayce implies in reading 1152-5.

In a well-rooted relationship with the divine flow of Cosmic Energy, no matter what the condition or "season" of life, the external circumstances need not disrupt, diminish, or decrease the life-giving power of the Source as it flows into our being. But first, the pattern and the practice must be established through meditation, prayer, and taking "delight" in the ways of the Divine.

One way to really get an understanding of the Tree of Life within you is to establish a relationship with one outside of you.

Take a walk in the woods and look for a special tree, a tree the Native American people might call a "grandfather tree." Usually this is a tree with many seasons of growth behind it that attracts you to it. When you find that tree, stand in front of it with your palms toward it.

Take a few deep breaths to clear your mind, and approach the tree respectfully. As you step toward it, notice when you begin to sense or feel the energy field of the tree. When you begin to sense the energy, stop and stand still for a few moments. Absorb its energy and be aware of any feelings and thoughts you are having. The energy field of the tree will interact with and stimulate your own subconscious. Consider it a message from the tree.

Now move closer and put your arms around it, so your chest and face are pressing on the trunk. Be respectful and nonjudgmental. Again, take a breath or two to clear your mind and be open to the communication from the tree. The "gift of life" can be in the form of intuitive perceptions, a healing and balancing of your energy, or other forms of subtle interaction with the tree.

And when it feels finished, step back from the tree and give thanks, always, for the experience it gave you. Depending upon your openness and receptivity, it may take several visits to the tree before something meaningful happens. But expect a result, and you may succeed on your very first try.

The Tree of Life is an image expressing the spiritual part of our being that is ever constant, never tires or grows weary, is always responsive and ever alive. It is an "upside down" tree that we connect with in meditation and bring to blossom in our bodies. Its roots are in heaven and its branches are in the earth.

As Jesus said, speaking *as the tree*, "I am the vine"— the connection to the Source— and we are the branches.

In all that he does, he prospers. (Ps. 1:3)

Prosperity is not merely a condition of material wealth or external possessions. In *Seven Spiritual Laws of Suc-*

cess, Deepak Chopra defines prosperity as the state of being happy. True prosperity is unconditional happiness. The conditon of Unconditional Happinesss bears an interesting connection to the "birthright" *of dominion.*

In *Pursuit of Happiness,* Dr. David Myers cites the results of his four essential qualities for happiness which he identified through a research project involving hundreds of people who considered themselves "happy." The research involved people from many different social, economic, and relgious and nonreligious backgrounds, and the goal was to identify the common demoninators in "happy" people. The essential characteristics the study identified are: self-esteem, optimism, extroversion, and a strong sense of personal control in their lives.

If your happiness depends on outward things instead of inner qualities, your happiness can be taken away from you, and thus is only conditional. *And the fruit of your joys will wither.*

A positive self-image, an optimisitc attitude toward life, the ability to relate and connect with people, and the sense of being in control of your thoughts and emotions is indeed a condition of prosperity. A happy person is likely to have a stronger immune system and to make better decisions in life.

Happiness is born of wisdom and truth, inner strength, integrity, and self-reliance; it will survive and deepen even during seasons of adversity, turmoil, and change. Delight in the ways of Spirit, for every experience in life yields its gold.

"The Lord abhorreth the quitter." (518-2)

Dr. George Lamsa, the translator of the Bible from the

Peshitta, the ancient Aramaic texts of the Eastern Ortho-
dox Christianity, renders "In all that he does he prospers," quite differently than the King James and all other
English translations of this verse.

In the Lamsa translation it reads: "Whatsoever he begins, he accomplishes."

In our lives, there are conditions which carry the
karmic pattern of completion. By this, I mean, there are
certain conditions—our "life issues"—which must be
healed and resolved. We often go from one thing to another in a manner of exploring and learning, and to leave
things "undone" here carries varying degrees of consequences from minor to major. But ultimately, as we go
through life, those big issues find us—we don't go looking for them—that are the very test of the soul. At this
point, we are face to face with the realization that this is
a condition to be met, to be healed, and it is not ever
going away until we complete the requirements to
change it.

With so many corporations, institutions, sports and
entertaiment mediums trying with all their creative
power and resources to capture our attention in order to
capture our money, keeping a sharp, clear focus on what
is really important in our lives and staying clear of the
distractions that fragment our energy and resources is a
major challenge. This is very similiar to the Sixth Challenge of Moses we covered earlier.

A test of our maturity is found in our reliability. Can
we be counted on to finish what we start?

With true wisdom, we will limit our commitments to
only those that are in harmony with our soul's purpose.

VISUALIZATION EXPERIENCE: BE LIKE A TREE

. . . make [it] the experience of self! 452-3

This exercise can be done indoors. All you need is a quiet space; some soft unintrusive music may help. And, if you choose, prerecord this exercise and play it back as you follow the meditation.

Take a few moments now to get comfortable. You may want to remove your shoes. Stand with your feet slightly apart, arms relaxed by your side. Or, if you prefer, sit down in a comfortable chair or lie down. Whatever suits you.

Close your eyes and take several slow, deep breaths to clear your mind and relax. Feel the relaxation coming in through the top of your head, through your nostrils, and into your lungs. With each inhalation, the feeling of relaxation expands until it fills you from head to toe, dissolving all stress, anxiety, and worry.

Now visualize a bright, bubbling stream. Its currents flow swiftly and strong. The water is clean and clear, the cleanest, clearest water you can imagine.

Now follow the stream as it flows through a landscape that is lush and well tended, fertile and fruitful, with abundant foliage and fruit growing along its banks. You feel the warmth of the sun. The earth is rich and fertile, and all that emanates from it radiates vitality and energy. The air is crisp and clean, textured with gentle breezes, and bird songs flow above the crystal stream. This is a perfect environment to grow and bloom and unfold in.

You are standing in the center, the very center of this place where all these energies converge at one holy and sacred place, the place where you are standing.

Now you see someone coming toward you, someone very wise. An aura of prosperity, happiness, of many blessings radiate from this person. Take a moment now and observe that person as he (or she) comes to you. This person is the keeper of this sacred place. Under his (or her) hands, everything blooms and grows.

The Keeper of the Garden approaches you. Your eyes meet, and as they do, the Keeper smiles and points to your feet. Be aware of your feet now touching the ground. And through your feet you become aware of earth, soft yet firm, rich with nutrients and fed by the sparkling sun-flecked, crystal stream that silently, smoothly flows through this lush and inviting land.

Now, with your eyes closed, feel your feet connecting to the earth like roots of a tree pushing deep into the soil and deeper, branching out, forking, dividing, creating webs of energy that draw nourishment and strength from the rich soil that flows up through your feet and fills your body.

You feel this energy as a warmth building in your body rising through your feet, through the ankles, over the knees, into the thighs, filling the lower abdominal area, rising up through the circulatory system, the lymph system, into the lungs, the heart, into the neck, into the brain cells, until your head, your whole body is filled with energy.

The Keeper smiles warmly, indicating great pleasure with how well you are doing with this experience. With just the lightest touch of a finger, he (or she) touches the top of your head. And suddenly you are aware of the light from the sun shining down, warming you with its great, life-giving energy. The energy of the earth and the sun mix and mingle within you, and as they do, your energy begins to extend out far beyond your body, like branches of a tree extending out from the trunk, pushing out, dividing, forking, creating new patterns and configurations, and all of them now are burgeoning with bright colored blossoms of great value and beauty.

Now you notice the garden is filled with people. Some you immediately recognize, and others you don't. And they are all astounded by the tree that you have become.

Some look to the Keeper of the Garden in awe at what flourishes so resplendently under his (or her) care. And others can't stop looking at you. They come closer, drawn by the energy radiating from you and the many different kinds of gifts that are extended from your branches. A small child comes and pulls a blossom from the lowest branch—you recognize the child—and behold as soon as it is plucked, another fruit exactly like it grows in its place. Someone else, someone much older, reaches up and picks another bright blossom. It's a gift from you to them. As soon as it is plucked, another grows in its place. More come, and every time something is picked, something else even more lovely grows in its place.

The Tree is ever blooming, ever giving, rooted in deep soil watered by the crystal stream.

The Keeper smiles again, delighted at how well you've done with this experience. In the Keeper's hand is a book. He (or she) turns the book, and you see the title imprinted in letters of gold. As he (or she) hands you the book, a strong breeze blows across the field, rattling the leaves of all the trees. The Keeper nods and turns away. The book is a gift to you, a reminder that you can come back to this Sacred Spot in this Garden of Life anytime, in any season, day or night. You know the way.

Take a nice deep breath. Slowly open your eyes, stretch your arms, wiggle your toes, and gently return to your normal consciousness, feeling alert and energized and fully capable of recalling this experience whenever it will serve you.

MEDITATE UPON THE MESSAGE

Did this experience as a Tree of Life help you in any way? How?

How would you describe the blossoms on your

branches? What do you relate them to in your own life?

Who was the child and what "fruits" did he or she pick from the tree? The older person? The other people?

Many people have been a "Tree of Life" to others. Some like Mother Teresa and Mahatma Ghandi have a dramatic and obvious impact on the world. Others are planted in smaller arenas, yet influence hundreds, thousands, perhaps millions of people. And some grow in smaller circles of community, family, work, and friends. What Trees of Life do you know?

What has been their impact on you?

In your journal, describe what it is like to be a Tree of Life to others.

A MESSAGE TO ME:

Use your journal to write, draw, or expand upon your own impressions.

Less Than Angels, One with God

PSALM 8

O Lord, our Lord, how majestic is thy name in all the
    earth!

Thou whose glory is above the heavens
is chanted by the mouth of babes and infants.
Thou hast found a bulwark because of thy foes,
to still the enemy and the avenger.

When I look at thy heavens, the work of thy fingers,
the moon and the stars which thou hast established;
what is Man that thou dost care for him?

Yet thou hast made him a little less than the angels,
and doest crown him with glory and honor.

Thou hast given him dominion over the works of thy
    hands;
thou has put all things under his feet,
all sheep and oxen, and also the beasts of the field,
the birds of the air and the fish of the seas,
whatever passes along the paths of the sea.

O Lord, our Lord, how majestic is thy name in all the
    earth!

P salm 8 is a glorification of Genesis, a wonderful paean to Creation and a restatement and reaffirmation of our place in it. The majesty of the poetry reconnects us to the wonderful vision of our Genesis birthrights and our opportunities to experience "Eden" every day through surprising moments of intuition or in meditation or simple appreciation for being alive. But most of all, the psalmist offers us a power point to again discover, affirm, and connect to our Divine Self-Awareness.

This psalm does not appear in any of the Bible study recommendations in the Edgar Cayce readings. Yet it is difficult not to include it as a power point because of its respect for creation and our relationship to the angels.

What is Man that thou dost care for him?
Yet thou hast made him a little less than the angels,
and doest crown him with glory and honor."

THE WISDOM OF THE EDGAR CAYCE READINGS

The will that makes the soul of man individual, and a little lower than the angels; yet when raised in the power that may be through the glorifying of the Son as to be one *with* the Son, one *with* the Father, and *thus* above the angels in glory. 439-2 As ye then forgive those who trespass, who speak evil, who are ungentle, who are unkind, so may the Father forgive thee when thou art wayward, when *thou* art headstrong and seek His Face. These are the laws. These are unchangeable. For He hath made thee a little lower than the angels, yet at no time hath He said to the angel, "Sit thou on my right side." 792-1 In the life, then, of Jesus we find the oneness made manifest through the ability to overcome all of the temptations of the flesh, and the desires of same, through making the *will one with the Father*. For as we find, oft did He give to those about Him

those injunctions, "Those who have seen me have seen
the Father," and in man, He, the Son of Man, became one
with the Father. Man, though the same channel, may
reach that perfection, even higher than the angel, though
he attend the God. 900-16 For he, man, has been made just
a little lower than the angels; with all the abilities to become *one with Him!* . . . 2172-1

What a glorious realization to know that we carry the
design of the Co-creator within us. It is a birthright. The
luminous, glorious presence of angels overshadow us
now! Whenever we feel small and puny, powerless and
victimized, we need to recall the vision of our potential
to be greater than the angel. There it is—we are less than
angels now, but with the birthrights and the pattern to
become One with the Divine—and thus, outshine the
angels in radiance and glory.

Theologically speaking, angels represent a different
order of Creation which interacts and intervenes in
our human/spiritual stream of evolution. Some angels
are described as being hundreds of feet, if not miles,
in height. Others are tiny, the size of parakeets and
peanuts. They come in all shapes and sizes, with marvelous powers and incredible timing and presence. They come
as agents of the Creator to assist us in our development.

Edgar Cayce defined angels as "dynamic laws" and
"energy systems" operating throughout the Universe
that influence and alter our consciousness and receptivity to spiritual influences.

Spiritually, we have clouded our ability to perceive
correct relationships, thus we, as humans, are "less than
the angels." Yet we retain within us the potential and the
ability to become one with the Source, one with the

whole, and still know ourselves to be ourselves, and thus above the angels. And it is for that purpose they watch over us and guide us. As we are souls bearing the divine image, our destiny is to know ourselves to be part of a loving, creative, healing, compassionate Spirit! The angels are there as agents of help and protection until that destiny is fulfilled.

LEARNING FROM THE ANGELS

The question to ask first is: *What is an angel?*
Have you ever been visited by an angel? Or dreamed of one?
Have you ever known someone who seemed like an angel?

It is your birthright and your heritage to know that indeed you are the center of a universe, and all the forces of Creation, including the angelic realm, are there to assist you in your development. The angels do this because of the Divine Image you carry within. Their purpose and desire is to assist you as you become more aligned and defined by what and who you really are!

Imagine what it feels like to be an angel—and communicate that feeling to another!

PSALM 8: PART TWO
CELEBRATING THE CREATION

The Cayce readings promise that, if one will get the spirit or the feeling of the Scriptures, that feeling will carry them to the gates of heaven. Isn't that a nice thought! In Psalm 8, the psalmist is enraptured by a sense of oneness with the glories of nature and experiences a mystical perception of his relationship with the Creative Forces.

When we comprehend the Psalms as "expressions of consciousness" which we most fully understand by connecting to the original experience of the psalmist that produces the song, then contemplation of the Eighth Psalm promises to be an exhilarating and joyous lesson.

The Fourth Principle or Commandment given in Exodus 20 is to honor the Sabbath. The commandment is also linked to the seven days of Creation, as if to imply that meditating on the six days of creation—or of Creation itself—is a key to "restoring the soul." Reflecting upon and meditating on the "very beginning" and the forces and processes revealed in the "days" or cycles of Creation is a powerful and effective way to reconnect to our spiritual roots and, perhaps, to an intuitive sense of our unique and special relationship with nature and the Heart of Love which has brought it and us into being.

The Native Americans invite us to go out into nature, any natural setting, and just sit and observe. Take no thought of identifying the local flora and fauna. Don't even close your eyes and use the restorative and balancing energies of nature to assist you in going inward to meditate. Rather, they suggest you continue returning regularly to the same spot through the changing seasons and simply observe. Over time, you will begin to feel very differently about the land and the environment, and a more connected and intuitive relationship with the sacredness of the environment will manifest.

All of nature gives evidence of divine intelligence. You see the wisdom of nature expressed as animals, insects, trees, seasons, order, and harmony. Something as big as the sky or as grand as a mountain or lake, or as small as a blade of grass, a grain of sand, or a pebble has evidence of the Creator in it. Consider the intricacies and the intelligence manifested in each thing you observe. As you observe, reflect, and meditate, be aware that this Great

Intelligence is the same power and spirit that made you and is mindful of you—as it is of the sparrows, the lilies, and all things.

As expressions of One Source, these are all your relations. Say hello and learn to love them. The psalmist perceives that he—as is all humankind—is the master and steward of the Creation. As free-willed, creative beings endowed with intelligence and the ability to choose, we have a unique and special relationship to the worlds around us.

We are the apex of Creation.

On the other hand, we are *made lower than the angels.*

We must raise our energy and our consciousness to be equal to our destiny.

EXPLORING THE SPIRIT OF THE EIGHTH PSALM: A NATURE WALK WITH A MYSTICAL EYE

Of course, there are many examples of nature producing expanded and mystical insights. You may want to use one or more of these as you experiment with using nature as a medium to expand your insights and relationship to the spirit of Psalm 8.

SUGGESTION FOR EXERCISES:

I am surrounded by miracles. Walt Whitman

How many miracles can you notice among the trees, in the flowers, in the water, across the sky?

What miracles are you experiencing for the first time as you focus your attention on the beauty around you?

In a sacred way I walk,
In beauty's way I walk.

In a sacred way I walk this earth.
Every step on Mother Earth is a prayer.
Native American Chant

Keep this prayer in mind as you walk through nature. Chant it silently or outloud. Learn to walk in nature— and through life—with a prayerful, respectful attitude toward the Creation, and a more profound and meaningful connection and relationship to God will bring healing, health, and a new appreciation of life and its possibilities to you.

Split a stick and see Jesus. First-century Gnostic koan

Snap a twig and look closely at the intricate patterns and stunning designs within—and discover evidence of the Creator in everything.

To behold all of heaven in a grain of sand
and all the earth in the face of a flower.
William Blake

A hologram of the cosmos exists in a tiny piece of sand. The face of the flower glows with evidence of the nature of its Creator. Stop and stoop low and the secrets of the universe are revealed.

The creation of a thousand forests are contained in
one acorn. Ralph Waldo Emerson

Hold an acorn or any seed in your hand. Roll it along your fingertips. Allow its vast potential and potency to speak to you. Then plant it in the ground and reflect on what you have done.

As you practice these meditations and develop your

own, you will become not only more conscious of the natural world around you but of your own inner nature as well. And may the same enveloping sense of the cosmos that inspired the psalmist carry you to "the gates of heaven," as the Cayce readings promised.

A GUIDED EXPERIENCE:
PSALM 8

Find a comfortable place, and for a few moments focus on these questions:

What is the primary feeling or emotion in the Psalm?

Can you think of a time in your life when you felt a similar way?

What event or occasion triggered those feelings?

Now close your eyes, take a few deep breaths, and feel those feelings again—focus on the feelings you can relate to in the psalm. And with your next breath, magnify those feelings. And imagine now angels are carrying you through the years, back through time, back through happy, joyful moments in your life, back through times of your most innocent and childlike faith and trust in God. Carried by these happy, joyful, innocent feelings, as you go back, the scene changes quickly, rapidly, like scenes in a play or a movie, and you go back effortlessly and easily further and further back in time, even beyond this lifetime. Passing before you now are people in costumes and settings of different eras, different cultures through the centuries. The changes occur with great speed, yet with remarkable detail until the scene slows down and stops, and you are looking down at a shepherd tending his flock in a great wilderness. The sky is a rich blue, the grass is green, and the air is clean and fresh. The flock is content as it grazes. The bell on the lead sheep tinkles occasionally, and their bleating sounds punctuate the silence.

Suddenly, a ray of golden light engulfs the shepherd. A smile grows across his face. You have eyes now to see what he cannot. Angels are around him. They glow with luminous hues, and their energy is loving and supporting. The shepherd cannot see them, but he realizes he is enveloped by something profound and spiritual. At the moment of this recognition, the very instant it comes into the shepherd's consciousness, a great, beautiful color swells out from his heart, and you know this is the work of the angels around him.

Suddenly the shepherd is excited, so happy now, suddenly so appreciative of just being alive. Now the words of a song begin forming in his mind. He has a small harp and begins singing.

With your next breath, you float down and become the shepherd looking out on the green fields, your heart full and open, surrounded by snowcapped mountains, birds darting overhead, and in the distance bleating and the tinkling of the bells on the sheep are heard. And you feel the song rising from your heart up through your throat.

A full feeling of joy and praise fills your body, so much so that even the angels begin to sing your song. You are aware now, more keenly than you ever have been before, of angels, of the presence of a loving spiritual force all around you. The words of a song are on your lips.

How does the song begin?

Take a few moments to listen, and when you are ready, take a few deep breaths, open your eyes slowly, and in your journal write down your impressions and the words of your song.

A MESSAGE TO ME:

Use your journal to write, draw, or expand upon your own impressions.

The Psalm of Attunement

Psalm 23

The Lord is my shepherd; I shall not want.
He maketh me to lie down in green pastures:
he leadeth me beside the still waters.
He restoreth my soul: he leadeth me in the paths of righteousness for his name's sake.

Yea, though I walk through the valley of the shadow of
death,
I will fear no evil: for thou art with me;
thy rod and thy staff they comfort me.

Thou preparest a table before me in the presence of mine
enemies:
thou anointest my head with oil; my cup runneth over.

Surely goodness and mercy shall follow me all the days
of my life:
and I will dwell in the house of the Lord for ever.

COMMENTARY

There is a long tradition of free translation and changing meanings of the psalms through the years, none more so than Psalm 23. The Twenty-third Psalm, or Shepherd's Psalm, is one of the best-known and most universally loved pieces of Scripture. It is a prayer that is common to the Jew, the Christian, the Buddhist, the Muslim, and the New Ager. If anybody knows any part of the Bible, it is most likely the Twenty-third Psalm.

For early Christians, this psalm was interpreted as prophetic of the Christ. For others, the opening stanza rephrases the archetype of the Promised Land. The imagery of lush, flowing sweet grass, clear, still waters, and the protective presence of a perfect companion speaks of that inward, centered space the seeker finds by turning within and heeding the voice of the true and deeper Self. It reminds us, we are only one breath away from Eden. For mystics and practitioners of the metaphysical or esoteric traditions, the "good shepherd" psalm is a perfectly phrased song of meditation and the mastery of one's thoughts.

Each of the psalms is a little treatise on meditation; Psalm 23, perhaps, the best of any in its simplicity and structure. Joel Goldsmith, the author of many best-selling books on mysticism and spirituality, considered it the perfect prayer because it is a song of affirmations, not petitions. The psalmist is confident of his relationship with the Source. He does not ask, beseech, or beg for divine favor; rather confidently, clearly, simply, succinctly, and with great depth affirms and expresses an assurance of the Divine.

So familiar and universal is the structure of the psalm that it has been adapted, both seriously and humorously, as the antidote for many situations. There is the Busy

Person's Twenty-third Psalm, the Native American Twenty-third Psalm, the Teacher's Psalm, the CEO's Twenty-third Psalm, the Harried Housewife's Psalm, the Gambler's Psalm, and so forth. Different writers find in the psalm a pattern they can identify with, update it with their own language and symbology, and make it their own. For an example, one recent version called *The Channel Surfer's Psalm* acknowledges the power of the "boob tube" in our lives:

The TV is my shepherd, I shall not want.
It makes me to lie down on the sofa.
It leads me away from the faith, and it destroys my
   soul.
It leads me in the paths of sex and violence for the
   sponsors' sake.

Yea, though I walk in the shadow of Christian responsibilities,
there are no interruptions, for the TV is with me.
Its cable and remote control, they comfort me.
It prepares a commercial for me in the presence of my
   worldliness.

It anoints my head with humanism and consumer-
   ism.
My coveting runneth over.
Surely laziness and ignorance shall follow me all the
   days of my life
and I shall dwell in the house watching TV forever.

This version is called *The Twenty-third Psalm for Busy People* and has a more positive tone:

The Lord is my pacesetter, I shall not rush.
He makes me stop and rest for quiet intervals,
He provides me with images of stillness, which restore
    my serenity.
He leads me in ways of efficiency; through calmness
    of mind,
and His guidance is peace.
Even though I have a great many things to accomplish
    each day,
I will not fret, for his presence is here,
His timelessness, His all importance will keep me in
    balance.
He prepares refreshment and renewal in the midst of
    my activity.

By anointing my mind with His oils of tranquillity.
My cup of joyous energy overflows.
Surely harmony and effectiveness shall be the fruits of
    my hours,
For I shall walk in the peace of my Lord, and dwell in
    His House forever.

There are thousands of stories that demonstrate the
place this psalm has in the hearts and souls of people.
For many, it is magic and powerful. When Roy Campa-
nella, the Brooklyn Dodgers Hall of Fame catcher, was
left paralyzed and in a wheelchair from an auto accident,
the psalm became a daily part of his therapy and ultimate recovery. "Mamma always said, chicken soup and
the Twenty-third Psalm could cure anything," he said.
    A captain in the U.S. Army in World War II kept a copy
of the Twenty-third Psalm with him throughout the war
and recited it as a daily devotion. He was convinced that
this practice was the reason he did not lose a single man
under his command. He acknowledged that the "good

shepherd" kept him and his men from the killing fields.
How could it be even more powerful and effective,
calm, centering, and soothing for you?

The Good Shepherd

The Wisdom of the Edgar Cayce Readings

Q. In the book Your Faith Is Your Fortune, *is Neville's commentary on the Twenty-third Psalm accurate?*
A. It is for Neville, but not for [you] . . . For, as the prayer,
as the 23rd Psalm is, "The Lord is *my* shepherd," not . . .
anyone else's, but *"my* shepherd." That is, *"I am the Lord's,*
for I hear His voice, heed His call." 2533-7

Cayce gives us a lot to think about in that little quote
from above. We are to heed the voice of our "shepherd"
and not someone else's. Our relationship to the Creative
Forces, to God, is intended to be personal and private,
intimate, and not through the recitation of collectively
held dogmas, creeds, and doctrines. To follow the shepherd, we have to know our own mind.

The image of the "good shepherd" is a biblical code
word for masters of their thoughts, according to Paul
Solomon, founder of the Fellowship of the Inner Light.
In a flock of sheep, there is always one sheep whom all
the others will follow, even if it leads them over a cliff.
The shepherd knows if he keeps that lead sheep out in
front, the rest of the herd will organize itself around her
and go wherever she goes.

Have you ever tried to watch your thoughts for a day?
Or even an hour. Or for a few minutes. At one level, our
thoughts go constantly toward our wounds, pulling us

toward our insecurities and feelings of loss and abandonment, and we develop fixated ways of thinking—a string of thoughts, looped together, that bring us back time and again to the same old ways of thinking and feelings we want to avoid.

In the days of the California gold rush, a group of pioneers eager to reach the gold fields gambled on outrunning the winter storms and got trapped by heavy snow while trying to cross the rugged Sierra Nevada Mountains. Lost in the wilderness, they all perished. The tragedy was they were always within easy reach of food and shelter. But they died walking in circles over their own footprints covered by the falling snow.

We can be just like that doomed party, going around and around in the configuration of our own thoughts, focusing on the experience of loss, failure, missed opportunities—and emptiness. In that mind-set, we can become so preoccupied with our own dilemmas that we don't even recognize that we have traveled this same empty, sterile, exhausted path before. We keep walking over our own footprints, trapped in the same old emotional loop again—with no rescue party coming to save us.

And at the same time, all the help we need is just a breath away. If we take an intentional breath, connect to the power of a higher self, suddenly we have the opportunity to "shepherd" our thinking in a new direction—toward sources of help and nourishment. We are literally surrounded by everything we need to heal, grow, and prosper, but it can be invisible and untasted by us because of our fixated ways of thinking.

The good shepherd keeps his "flock of thoughts" in order, always alert, keeping the wolves at a distance, and is ever mindful where the green grass and still waters—the sources of renewal and refreshment—can be found.

He restoreth my soul:
He leadeth me in the paths of righteousness
For His name's sake. (Ps. 23:3)

THE WISDOM OF THE EDGAR CAYCE READINGS

Not a sectarian awakening; not a dogmatic awakening—
but that of the same truths as is set forth in "The meek
shall inherit the earth—The pure in heart shall see God."
He that is grounded in the truths as set forth here is
grounded indeed in the truths that makes the individual
one with, in will and purport, the whole creative energy,
and will make for that individual the faith that moves
mountains and maketh the pastures green where there
was consternation and trouble before. 254-48

*"Blessed are they who delight in the laws of the Lord,
and on his law they meditate both day and night."*
Meditation creates nourishment for the soul. It provides energy to the organs and adds life to the body.
Moses found manna in the wilderness. "My soul is restored," states the psalmist. Jesus says, "I have food ye
know not of."
As shepherds, our lead thought needs to be a trust
thought, a wisdom thought, a love thought—and then
we need to "shepherd" our energies so all the subsequent
thoughts follow. We need to shepherd our thoughts so we
are always close to the "still waters," the source of renewal and the "green pastures," the source of strength.

Yea, though I walk through the valley
of the shadow of death. (Ps. 23:4)

THE WISDOM OF THE EDGAR CAYCE READINGS

He that walketh in the light, and purposes in his heart to *do, be,* that which *the* Creative Forces would *have* one be, shall *not* be *left* alone! for though he walk through the valley of the shadow of death, His arm, His hand, will direct thy ways. His rod, His staff, will comfort thee! Though they walk through green pastures, or in the ways that lead down to the sea, yet His Spirit, His arm, His face, will *comfort* thee in the *way* thou goest!

When one, then, is so guarded, so guided, *indeed* for a *purpose,* is one kept in the way! 1909-3

The reality of death is that we are eternal beings, we live forever. The "shadow of death" is fear, and fear is an illusion born of false beliefs. Death in the body is a birth in the spiritual. In sleep, we die a little death; in meditation, we taste a portion of eternity.

By moving our mind from its usual involvement with external reality and breaking the loop of our fixated thinking and directing it inward, we go into that "thick darkness where God is." The darkness means confronting the dim and often foreboding areas of the repressed subconscious.

The image of going through the valley means that there is often a journey between those wonderful moments when we experience the complete and total realty of the Divine. But having tasted it, our body and soul remembers, and if we permit, we return to it again and again.

As we carry out our ideals and commitments and find our way back to a fully integrated relationship with the Light, we must open up and face many dark areas of the soul. The walk through the valley of the shadow of death is the period of the "middle passage" when that which was no longer is and that which is to be has not yet come. The "in-between time" separates the seed from the blossom. It is the "in-between time" when we are no longer who we used to be, but not yet who we are to become.

Western people, Americans in particular, have a fear of opening themselves to the contents of their own unconscious. And rightly so, because so few of our institutions prepare us to adequately deal with what we find there. And yet in the Twenty-third Psalm, we find the perfect pattern. There is always light on both sides of the darkness.

In meditation, we evoke the power and protection of a higher spiritual power—a Good Shepherd. As the centering process continues and we open up to the deeper mind, we must pass through the various layers of the subconscious mind where all our repressed, denied, and painful memories have been compacted. Many people are afraid of any practice that "stills the mind" because it allows buried, troublesome, and unresolved feelings to rise into consciousness. The first thing they encounter when all the distractions are reduced or removed is everything that they have pushed down to "keep the peace" by staying busy and in denial. When these rejected feelings start to surface, they seem to confirm what we may have feared all along—I really am a worthless, weak piece of discarded trash after all!

However, it is not death itself, but the *shadow* of death, the fear of death, the illusion of death that the shepherd guides his thoughts through. As often as we repeat the psalm and anchor it into our nervous system with strong feelings of confidence and assurance, we are rerouting the neuropathways in the brain and training them to revert to this pattern of confidence and assurance when faced with the "fears of death" that are wrapped up in issues of abandonment, betrayal, loss, and powerless-ness. These issues are the "wolves and bandits and wild dogs" from which the Good Shepherd protects his flock.

There is an Intelligence within you that knows this terrain very well. Keep your mind on Spirit, and you will get through to the other side. When you do, there you are! The table is spread before you. Eventually we come to realize the only enemies we have are the fear, doubt, anger, jealousy, and resentments we create. They stay alive inside us as long as we feed and sustain them with our energy. If we starve them long enough by putting our attention elsewhere, eventually they lose their power and dissipate.

Or we could say it another way—our only enemy is that energy, or principle, which keeps us out of alignment with the Divine. And when the "principle" is recognized as an initiator for our soul lessons, it is no longer an enemy, but a teacher and friend.

Thou anointest my head with oil. (Ps. 23:5)

THE WISDOM OF THE EDGAR CAYCE READINGS

Q. Have I any healing power?
A. What power *hasn't* the body, with that faith, with that *understanding!* These may be used in *many* directions by the laying on of hands, and with prayer—anointing as of oil—as has been given, anointing with oil—pouring in of those of the spirit, that knowledge, of understanding—will bring *blessings* to many. Do not *neglect* that that has been committed into thy keeping . . . 2112-1

Among the desert nomads in the Holy Land, one could never be sure of the intention of a stranger. Was he friend or foe? The custom was to take the stranger to the tent of the chieftain to be questioned and evaluated while he enjoyed the chieftain's hospitality. A meal was prepared, and cups would be placed before them. After some discussion and probing, the chief would make a determination. If the stranger was deemed to be a friend, the stranger's cup was filled to overflowing, and he was invited to eat. If the chief remained suspicious and uncertain of the stranger's motives, the cup remained empty, and he was treated as an enemy.

Don't be a stranger to meditation, and come as a friend to the tent of the Lord.

The shepherd's staff, Cayce indicates, is a representation of the flow of energy that is raised in meditation. It rises first from the ground, to the gonads, or root chakra, at the base of the spine, ascends up the spine and flows upward to the thyroid, the seat of the will, at the neck, and then to the pineal at the crown of the head, and flows into the pituitary, activating this master gland. The brain instantly secretes its pain-killing, pleasure-enhancing endorphins and feelings of "goodness and mercy" follow.

This same representative flow of energy is seen also in the story of the enlightenment of the Buddha. He spent many years meditating under the branches of the bodhi tree. One day, a great storm occurred, and the ground opened up, releasing a giant seven-headed cobra that rose up behind the Buddha and spread its hood over him like an umbrella to protect him. This was his moment of enlightenment.

Thy rod and thy staff—and in this case, thy serpent— they comfort me.

This psalm, too, has something to tell us about being

sheep and being priests. We can remain content as sheep, finding a voice within to keep us close to our comfort zones, where food and water are found. Yet for those who are willing to take the "dark journey" another level of reality is to be gained—symbolized as being an honored and anointed guest in the House of the Lord. The passage in the dark valley suggests that we cannot always be connected to the sources of refreshment in our thinking—that there are often long lapses when we must cross dry, hostile, unsupportive spiritual and emotional landscapes before we reach another oasis, and we just have to make it through.

Anointing is part of the ancient ritual of being recognized and accepted for priesthood. To be anointed, not by an external ritual, but by the increased flow of energy that follows through the mastery of your thought processes and their connection to your emotional well-being, makes you indeed a special treasure, a special possession as promised in Exodus 19.

EXERCISES IN PSALM CREATIVITY

Either alone, or with your Bible study group, meditate upon the psalm and then "translate" it into your own experience. Using first-person, affirmative statements, rewrite the psalm in language and images from your own life and direct experience. Few of us have any daily contact with shepherds, yet we all need to find an organizing principle or function that gives meaning to our lives. Although the good shepherd is a rich, historical, and familiar image, how would you translate it into a "felt" image of your own?

What is it in your life that gathers and leads your thought processes the most? And where does it take you?

How would you describe to someone from another

planet who or what a shepherd is or does?

Speak the psalm aloud, and feel the feelings. Yogananda suggests you begin working with the sacred literature by voicing it as loudly as you can. This gives energy and power to your study, and any exaggeration helps get the attention of the subconscious. Voice it out loud and know what you are affirming.

Take each line apart, and render the allusions and images into specific instances and areas of your life. Remember *The Channel Surfer's Psalm*. Make it serious or humorous!

Describe the experience that resonates with lying down in green fields, or drinking cool waters?

What does it feel like to be a sheep in the care of a good shepherd? A lazy or distracted shepherd?

What are some of the scariest, darkest days of your life? How did you get through them?

In your life, what could the experience of "anointing" relate to? Self-validation? Self-honoring? Being known by others even as you know yourself?

AN EXPERIMENT WITH THE MORPHOGENIC FIELD

The theory of the morphogenic field states that when a sufficient number of people have focused their attention on a new idea, the energy of the collective reaches a critical mass, the idea expands, and its accessibility is enhanced. More and more people can engage more easily with the idea.

Because Psalm 23 has been so well known and loved throughout the ages, its morphogenic field should be quite large and vibrant, making it very easy to memorize and understand. To explore this theory, try this little experiment.

Get a group of people—children or adults who have not

memorized the psalm. The more unfamiliar they are with it, the better. Divide them into two groups. Have one group attempt to memorize the psalm, so it can be recited, and the other group work with a psalm of approximately the same length but not as familiar or universal. If the theory of the morphogenic field is correct, the group memorizing the Twenty-third Psalm should complete the assignment much faster than the other group.

Another variation is to have the same child or individual memorize the two psalms and then see which one was easier to memorize.

Then question the person about the meaning of each psalm. Ideas and feelings related to the Twenty-third Psalm should be much more accessible and flowing.

And, of course, have fun while you are doing it.

Song of Endless Wealth
and Attitude Adjustment

Psalm 24

The Earth is the Lord's, and the fullness thereof;
The world, and they that dwell therein.
For he hath founded it upon the floods.

Who shall ascend into the hill of the Lord?
or who shall stand in his holy place?

He that hath clean hands, and a pure heart; who hath not
    lifted up his soul unto vanity, nor sworn deceitfully.
He shall receive the blessing from the Lord,
And righteousness from the God of his salvation.

This is the generation of them that seek Him,
That seek thy face, O Jacob. Se'lah.

Lift up your heads, O ye gates; and be ye lift up,
Ye everlasting doors; and the King of glory shall come in.

Who is this King of glory? The Lord strong and mighty,
  the Lord mighty in battle.
Lift up your heads, O ye gates;
even lift them up, ye everlasting doors; and the King of
  glory shall come in.
Who is this King of glory?
The Lord of hosts, he is the King of glory. Se'lah.

The Wisdom of the Edgar Cayce Readings

Q. I seek direction as to how to clear my debts.

A. These can be met only by measuring up to that
which brings the promise—that is well known in self—
from the *source* of supply—materially, physically.

For the earth is indeed the Lord's, and the fullness
thereof. The silver and the gold are His. When ye measure to that standard where there is needed such for the
best mental and soul development, such is—will be—
supplied. 877-29

*Q. What will be the safest way for me to protect my surplus
money?*

A. This depends upon what it is protected for! This depends upon what is thy purpose, what is thy aim, what is
thy desire . . . look within self and see. Know that money,
as name, may take wings and fly away—unless used or
applied in that which gives reverence, and shows appreciation, and applies self as well as money in appreciation
of those sources from which it came. And the earth is the
Lord's, and the silver and the gold are His, as are the cattle
on the hills.

Then, with whom would you invest same? that thine
own body might be satisfied? Or that thou might be protected in thine old age?

Who giveth thee life? Seek the Lord while He may be
found; for He alone giveth that as brings peace and happiness and harmony in the experience of the entity.

And thus, as ye study to show thyself approved unto

Him, the way may be opened and shown thee . . . in which ye may use thyself, thy means, thy surplus, yea, thyself. Be happy to give thy surplus, to give *thyself*, to thy God! 1965-1 For to those whom the Lord loveth, and to those that give expressions of same, does the glory not only of the earth, but of the mental, of the spiritual things, become as a portion of their experience; not alone out of the earth but *within* same. For the earth is the Lord's and the fullness thereof is His to give to those that use its storehouse for the making known of the love of God to His children. 1032-1 . . . thy purpose in the world is *not* as a proof or as the justification of self, but rather to *glorify* that influence, that force, that power which gave thee being, gave thee conscious expression! Hence in thy dealings with thy fellow men, bring hope—not for that so much of the material gain, for the earth is the Lord's and the fullness thereof. Then, live holy and right in His ways and purposes—the *supply*, the abundance will be the result of thy fulfilling the law of supply in the experience of someone else! 1946-1 If there would be more and more coordination of the oneness of all, rather than the differences, how well may "the earth and the fullness thereof" be understood by those who know the glory of the Lord through combining these, rather than seeking differences! 1217-1 For His ways are not past finding out to those that would *do right* and justice to their fellow man! Know that the earth *is* the Lord's and the fullness thereof, and His promises have been that there is abundance for all that keep and know His ways to dwell therein—and that the seed of such shall *not* beg bread. 391-16

For individuals suffering financial hardships or concerned with fulfilling economic responsibilities—Cayce invariably turned to the opening verse of the Twenty-fourth Psalm to correct their thinking and resolve

their fears: *The earth is the Lord's, and the fullness thereof.*
The Christ Consciousness—the first consciousness—is the perfect awareness of correct relationships in spiritual aspects.

> He, that Christ Consciousness, is that first spoken of in the beginning when God said, "Let there be light, and there was light." 2879-1 The Light became the light of men—Mind made aware of conscious existence in spiritual aspects or relationships as one to another. 1947-3

To understand that we are in the Image of God and that the earth and all that it contains comes from the same Source that we do is to begin to reestablish proper relationships. As is sometimes said, God owns everything; and we are His heirs. We claim our inheritance, not when we die, but when we come alive.

In many ancient spiritual traditions from the Greeks to the Native Americans, the earth is an entity, a consciousness they call Mother. The Mother supplies their needs and in her bosom is the balm for all sorrow, pain, and injury.

In Exodus, the command to "honor the Sabbath" is linked to the six days of Creation. A proper Sabbath meditation, one that is guaranteed to renew our spirits and give us strength, is to reconsider our relationship to the earth and to the Source which created us in the beginning. The earth is an expression of God's love. Every aspect of its incredible diversity bears the imprint of Divine Intelligence. There is a "fullness" that fills the Universe, even the places that we perceive as empty are filled with the substance of the Divine, the creative "stuff" of manifestation.

When negative emotions get triggered, and stress begins to overwhelm our nervous system, when we begin to worry about not having enough, we experience immediate poverty—a poverty of spirit, because we are diminishing our own strength and shrinking our connection to abundant energy of the Divine which supports us. When our thoughts lead us into fear of lack and scarcity, it is time to be still, know, and affirm the "fullness of the Lord."

In the Bible, water is a mystical code word for Spirit. The image of water is often used by artists and poets to depict an initial stage in the processes of the Unseen Forces or Spirit becoming matter. In Genesis, a great "mist" rises from the earth. This psalm proclaims the earth is founded *upon the seas* and *established upon the floods.* The allusion to seas and floods points to a higher level of reality: to the "reservoir and flow" of Spirit.

The ancient worldview perceived reality as a ladder or vertical chain stretching from the spiritual realms, down through the cosmos, through the stars and planets down into the visible, manifested forms of the earth. Without changing its own inherent essence of nature, each link of the chain or rung of the ladder produced the realm immediately below it. The lower realm, or link, was infused with the emanations or vibratory frequencies of the higher dimensions above it. Thus everything in the realm of earthly form and matter was an expression—a shadow or copy—of a higher reality just above it.

By working with and observing the external reality which we can see—a flowing river, an ocean, a calm lake—we can profoundly connect to the inner images which we cannot see. Carl Jung named these patterns as archetypes, and compared them to dry riverbeds in the psyche. When the connection between the outer image and its corresponding inner reality is made, the flow of psychic or spiritual energy is released. The vital, life-enhancing currents flow into and fill these ancient riverbeds of the soul and the psyche is renewed, re-enegerized, healed, and made whole. Green grass and flowering fields line the river banks, and the whole psyche begins to prosper.

The goal or value of meditation is to stimulate the flow of vital energy through the body systems. Having an outer image as a mental focus or ritual space that resonates with the inner structure or spiritual pattern is a valuable aid for redirecting this flow of psychic and spiritual energy upward for spiritual perception and inner healing. As we raise the energy, contact the higher realms, we become more aware of subtle energy patterns and, through our bodies, become sources through which that power becomes manifested on the earth.

The earth is indeed, as the psalmist sang, founded upon an ocean of Spirit, and its current runs through us and as us.

The images in the following stanzas of the psalm are replete with meditative overtones and provide additional power points to stimulate the flow of energy upward.

> Who shall ascend into the hill of the Lord
> or who shall stand in his holy place? (Ps. 24:3)

The hill, the mountain, the high place all represent the attainment of meditation—to reach that secret place, hidden and removed from ordinary consciousness, where the Divine Energy meets, intersects and illuminates the receptive mind and body.

Who shall ascend into the hill of the Lord?   For an answer, we could reflect back to the power points of Exodus 19:5 and and the dramatic images of Moses and the mountain in the last half of Exodus 20. Or we could turn ahead and reflect upon the experience of Jesus on the

Mount of Transfiguration (Matthew 17, Mark 9, Luke 9). Or we could look within.

The psalm answers its own question. The one who ascends is the one whose hands are clean and whose heart is pure. Jesus said, *Be ye perfect, even as my Father in heaven is perfect.* (Mt. 5:48) But who can be as perfect as God? Or as pure as Moses or Jesus. We can—through the purity of our intentions, the purity of the ideal we uphold we can have a perfect relationship to Spirit.

Hands symbolize our ability to be in control and to take action and our ability to give and receive. The person with clean hands and a pure heart is not meditating or seeking a connection with the Divine for ego enhancement, personal gain, or to get an advantage over others. When our hands are clean, our actions are not controlled by resentment, jealousy, intolerance, and hate. When our heart is pure, our motivations are not directed by self-centered, selfish, or self-indulgent imaginations. In that state, we have indeed become "perfect."

When our hands are clean and our heart is pure, we can "ascend into" the ever-present, self-renewing, inflowing Presence that is the high hill of the Lord.

Lift up your heads, O ye gates . . . (Ps. 24:7)

To fully appreciate the experience behind the imagery of the final stanza, we again recall that the body is both temple and mountain. The ancient temples of Egypt, Greece, and Israel were built in many ways to "the measure of Man." The outer court, the inner court, and the Holy of Holies of Solomon's Temple corresponds to the ordinary everyday conscious mind, subconscious mind, and superconscious, or higher mind. The precinct of the outer court is where the public mingled, including the Gentiles and the money-changers. This court relates to the conscious mind and our involvement in the outer world. All kinds of thoughts pass through, both clean and unclean, positive and negative. The inner court relates to the subconscious mind. In the inner court the priest made preparations for service. The priest performed ritual cleansing by bathing, donning the ritual robes, and prepared himself mentally and spiritually. This relates to our own inner preparations for meditation. We have to "come in" from the cares and concerns of everyday life, clean up our thinking by focusing on our purpose for meditating, eliminate distracting thoughts, and bring our awareness to a single focus—of making contact with the Divine.

The most sacred place of the temple was the Holy of Holies. Here on the most solemn and holiest day of the year, the High Priest entered to plead for forgiveness for the sins of people and to receive judgments from the Divine.

The Holy of Holies within us is the sacred place where we have conscious contact with the Divine. It is not a place we can ever enter into casually or without the proper spiritual preparations—our hands and hearts must be clean.

Open up, you ancient gates! In the temple there was a succession of doorways that led one from the busy outer courts of commerce and secular interactions. The doors opened into deeper and deeper recesses of the temple compound, through areas dedicated to the preparation and sacrifice, to areas of greater stillness and quiet, and then to the most sacred, dedicated area of all—the place of emptiness and peace, a place shed of all forms and manifestation, the innermost chamber where God was.

In the stillness of our minds, we invite an energy in, and it enters through ancient gates, the doorway of the soul, or higher mind—the chakra centers.

Within the energy systems that make up the physical

body there are points of contact through which the higher vibratory forces of Spirit make contact with the self. These points of contact, according to the Edgar Cayce readings, are located in the endocrine system, or ductless glands of the body.

The seven major endocrine glands are the pituitary, the pineal, thyroid, thymus, adrenals, cells of Leydig, and generative system.

Their counterpoints in the spiritual body are called chakras. Chakras are constellations of light and energy, or wheels, that operate in and through the subtle bodies on the astral, etheric, and spiritual planes.

The seven major chakras are identified as the third eye, the crown, the will center, the heart, the emotional center, the center of imagination, and the root chakra.

The chakras and their relationships to the endocrine system are:

THIRD EYE	PITUITARY
CROWN	PINEAL
WILL	THYROID
HEART	THYMUS
EMOTIONAL	ADRENALS
IMAGINATION	CELLS OF LEYDIG
ROOT	GONADS

In the model of the Hebrew Tree of Life (or in the Christian image of the descending dove) the energy enters from the top, the crown center, and flows down through the centers in the form of a lightning flash down to the lowest, most dense, and concrete form of the energy, which, in the body, manifests in the gonads, or reproductive system.

In meditation, as we invite this power in, we must also raise up the energy from the sexual center through the

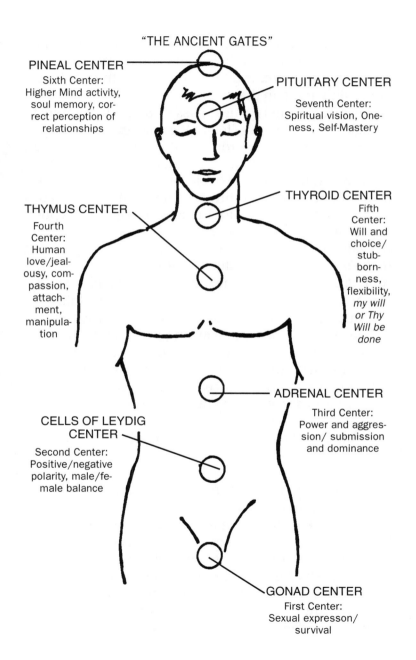

"THE ANCIENT GATES"

PINEAL CENTER
Sixth Center:
Higher Mind activity,
soul memory, cor-
rect perception of
relationships

PITUITARY CENTER
Seventh Center:
Spiritual vision, One-
ness, Self-Mastery

THYMUS CENTER
Fourth
Center:
Human
love/jeal-
ousy, com-
passion,
attach-
ment,
manipula-
tion

THYROID CENTER
Fifth
Center:
Will and
choice/
stub-
born-
ness,
flexibility,
*my will
or Thy
Will be
done*

ADRENAL CENTER
Third Center:
Power and aggres-
sion/ submission
and dominance

**CELLS OF LEYDIG
CENTER**
Second Center:
Positive/negative
polarity, male/fe-
male balance

GONAD CENTER
First Center:
Sexual expresson/
survival

chakras to the third eye, or pituitary. As the energy rises up, it activates each of the seven centers and the issues connected to them. It must rise through the levels and issues illustrated in the diagram.

Because the energy must pass through the centers to a single-minded point of focus, the analogy of the body as "sacred mountain" is apropos of the meditation process.

As the mind is still and focus narrows, the activity of the centers, the chakra wheels, open and expand as increased energy passes through them, "lifting" the consciousness of the meditator to higher levels of perception and awareness. At an internal and metaphysical level, the gates and ancient doors of this psalm are a reference to the opening of the centers as the energy rises from the root, or genital area, to the higher centers located at the throat and crown and then into the "holy of Holies" of the pituitary/third eye center. It is not unusual for people, in the process of learning to meditate, to actually hear the sound of creaking doors or rusty hinges as they work with opening long-closed spiritual centers. Others can actually produce a "pop" sound at each center as they raise the energy through the chakra system.

And be ye lift up, ye everlasting doors . . . (Ps. 24:7)

"Lift up your heads, O ancient gates, and be lifted up, ye ancient doors," voiced as an affirmation, is actually a way of speaking to the chakra system. Every cell in our body possesses intelligence, and when cells cluster sufficiently, they form a center which also possesses an intelligence which governs its functioning and coordinates its activities with all the other systems of the body.

Our entire body is a system of intelligences. At one time it was believed that the neurons associated with abstract thinking were located in a small area of the brain located at the base of the cerebral cortex. Now identical brain cells have been located through the entire body system—in the lymph glands, the heart, and even the skin. Our entire body is a living, thinking organism capable of storing memories and responding to suggestion.

Each cell of our body has intelligence, a mind of its own—and the cluster of cells forming a center is also governed by an intelligence which coordinates its function with other systems of intelligence within the body.

By affirming strong, positive statements charged with spiritual energy, we can actually direct the body to function according to its spiritual purpose and design. As we attune our conscious minds to the deeper mind, our words and intentions are infused with a spiritual force which can quicken the slower, denser energies of the material body. The energy from the highest link in the chain of creation flows into the lowest link, retaining its original essence while changing its form.

Lift up your heads suggests an expansion, an enlargement must occur before the higher energies, or spiritual patterns, are able to enter into our consciousness and manifest in and through the body.

And the King of glory shall come in. (Ps. 24:7)

Also the Levites which were the singers, all of them ... arrayed in white linen, having cymbals and psalteries and harps, stood at the east end of the altar, and with them an hundred and twenty priests sounding with trumpets:

It came even to pass, as the trumpeters and singers were as one, to make one sound to be heard in praising and thanking the Lord; and when they lifted up their voice with the trumpets and cymbals

and instruments of music, and praised the Lord, say-
ing, For he is good; for his mercy endureth for ever:
that then the house was filled with a cloud, even the
house of the Lord; so that the priests could not stand
to minister by reason of the cloud: for the glory of the
Lord had filled the house of God.

(2 Chronicles 5:12-14)

Who is this king of glory? This is as significant a question as the one raised by Jesus: "Who do men say that I
am?" If we don't have a workable concept of who or what
God is, how can we truly and fully understand the Image
in which we are made, or engage in enlightened divine
co-creation?

Our modern sensibilities may not fully appreciate the
war god luster of the Divine as "strong and mighty in battle."
Yet, we must also accept the fact that until we can quell
the conflicts raised by our own dual natures and life issues, we are constantly waging battles within ourselves.

By raising the ideal in meditation our vibratory rate is
quickened and, when the "high place" is reached, all limited thinking, all limited belief systems disappear, and
the brain releases its pleasure-producing/painkilling endorphins. "Goodness and mercy" follow and the power
and presence of the Divine fills the temple.

Isn't it reassuring to know that all our battles are decided in favor of "the unconquerable Light" when we invite it in?

A TEMPLE EXPERIENCE

The purpose of this meditation is to help facilitate an
in-depth experience inspired by the *spirit* of Psalm 24.

Find a comfortable spot. Close your eyes, relax. Take a

few more relaxing breaths, and notice where any tension or stress is being held in the body. Breathe into it and let it go.

As you relax, visualize your breath as a key to your soul. Each breath opens a door that takes you deeper. Each breath fits perfectly with the thoughts, the feelings you are experiencing, that are carrying you deeper and deeper to a place of stillness and quiet, where time and space and the restrictions of ordinary consciousness are dissolved.

Continue breathing in a relaxed, conscious manner, going deeper, to a memory, a memory of music, the most beautiful, special, sacred music you have ever heard—a time, perhaps, when you seemed to be lifted out of time and space by the power of a song, a sonata, a symphony, a choir. Allow the feelings that are so enjoyable, so sacred, and transcendent to carry you back even farther from your concerns, your worries, and cares. Release, relax, let go. Allow the music to lift you higher and higher, until you are lifted beyond all other sounds, and the music becomes a deep, resonant, rolling sound—the hum of creation. Feel it now, growing deeper, more rich and resonant throughout your entire body, in every cell, until you and this deep, rich tone are one.

And then there is stillness. Perfect quiet, perfect peace.

You are alone now, in the stillness of this sacred space, a high place, a holy place, a temple on a mountain high above the world. The temple compound is silent, except for the sound of splashing water in the fountain. Looking out you see great vistas of space, and you can see the patterns of cities and roads and villages below you. And the only sound you hear is the water splashing in the fountain.

You go to the fountain now and wash your hands. The water is refreshingly cool and clean. As you wash your hands you think about recent choices you have made and the actions you have taken, and your ability to give and receive. You keep your hands in the fountain until they feel clean.

And now you are aware of your heartbeat. Listen now. Your eyes are closed, and with the next breath, your heart begins to speak to you. What does your heart say? Is it happy? Is it sad? Is it comfortable with your motivations, the nature of your desires, your relationships?

Look within and listen. Is there anything to keep you from entering the temple. Release it and let it go. Continue releasing until your heart feels uncluttered, clear, clean, relaxed.

If you are experiencing difficulty or feeling blocked, there is a master—priest or priestess—or even an angel who has been assigned to help you. Allow them to approach. Invite their help.

The doors of the temple swing open silently, revealing a long hallway of marble and gold lit by torches and shafts of sunlight streaming through openings evenly spaced along the walls. Deep, rich overtones of voices chanting sacred sounds fill the temple with the feeling of sacred presence.

At the end of the hallway, a stairway rises up like a great rainbow with seven colors, with seven steps for every color.

The first steps are red, a very vibrant, beautiful red.

As you put your foot on the first red step, the energy of red begins to fill your body. You feel it rising up from your legs. The energy grows stronger, more complete with the next step, and the next. What is the energy of red like, and how does it feel as you take your next step and your next up the seven red steps. The energy of red is powerful, and you must use it wisely or great harm can come. Or great good.

Now there are seven steps of orange. The color is pure

and bright, a mixture of red and yellow. As you step on the very first orange step, the energy of red begins to change, and your body feels the change. Change is necessary, and as you take each step up the orange stairs, you know that you must change. You know what it is you need to release, to let go. What old ideas, habits, beliefs that you carry are no longer needed. Your heart is pure, your hands are clean, and so you accept the energy of change and continue along the steps of orange.

Seven steps of pure bright yellow now lie before you. Suddenly, all the changes feel complete, and you are filled with the energy and optimism of a new beginning. The energy of the first bright yellow step begins to spread through your body. The energy grows brighter and more intense, more pleasureful and satisfying with each step. Your thoughts are clear. Your mind is alert. You feel optimistic, enthusiastic, invincible. The very breath you breathe seems charged with this energy, and you breathe in deeply now and the energy expands with each breath.

You know you can stop with any of these feelings, on any of the stairs.

You choose to continue. And so you step up through the field of yellow energy until you reach the seven steps of green.

Bright, beautiful, pure steps of green now stand before you, the purest and most beautiful green you have the ability to imagine. Now imagine a green even more beautiful, the green of healing and growth, the green of prosperity and abundance, of green summer days and luxuriant summer growth. As you rise, you review things you have loved. Old memories of people and events come back to you with a feeling of appreciation for the lessons and the support they brought with them. And you are aware of many opportunities for growth and prosperity that were presented to you, some of which you accepted and many that you turned away. As you continue to rise up the path of the green stairs, the past and the present flow through you without emotional involvement or attachment. It feels good to realize again that you have been loved, you are loved, and you give love.

As you reach the last of the seven green steps, you realize now that you are ready to go up higher to the seven stairs of blue. You stop to admire the rich blue color of the seven stairs, so rich and blue it seems that stars shine from their luster. Below you the choir of white-robed beings stand in silence; there is no sound, only the muted, humming vibration from their presence.

You now begin on the stairs of the deep blue. A profound feeling of relaxation greets you. A sense of calmness and self-control begins to envelop you. The clarity and focus of the yellow stairs and the feelings of love and support of the green stairs now give way to a deep knowing within you, as if the choice to take your next step is being made for you, by another presence inside you that is deep and profound and all knowing—and where it leads, you are absolutely sure is to something healthy and whole and very good. Memories float and drift through your consciousness. You have dim memories of what it feels like to resist this deep mind with your personal will and choose harder paths than this one. And you are comforted now by where you are and what you know, and you take another step even higher.

The darkness of deep indigo lies before you. You can no longer see the temple or the choir below you. There is no fear, for this indigo darkness is a comforting presence, and here deep memories begin to rise in your awareness—of old, forgotten choices and young devotions, even memories of former lifetimes, even of lives in other dimensions—and now there is a most profound sense of your spiritual self. You feel as if you have now risen above your physical self into the realm of the divine image that is who you really are. And curiously, there is still a dim memory of a time when you believed that all you were was a physical body.

The darkness gives way now to the next color. The energy of violet radiates from the stairs in front of you and permeates your energy field, extending and expanding your awareness beyond your furthest thought—until you feel an incredible oneness and identity with all of creation. You are one with it all. Each step up the violet stairs brings new depth to the understanding of god, of divine mind, of holy breath, of sacred energy.

As you reach the seventh lavender step, a brilliant, beautiful radiant white light floods over you. You are bathed in white Light. You feel it in your mind, you feel it in your emotions. Your spirit is totally cleansed. The cells, atoms, and tissues of your body are totally restored. Your whole being now resonates to the vibrations of the Divine Image. The Crowning Glory has come to you.

Now the voices of the choir can be heard again, with a song of joy and praise. It is time to come back, down the stairs retaining all the experiences of the seven colors of the seven steps, down the torch-lit, sun-filled hallways, out past the fountain, and back again to where you are in the present.

Wiggle your toes, stretch your arms, and when you are ready, open your eyes slowly.

Return now.

A MESSAGE TO ME:

Use your journal to write, draw, or expand upon your own impressions.

Prayer of Protection

PSALM 91

He who dwells in the shelter of the Most High, who abides in the shadow of the Almighty, will say to the Lord, "My refuge and my fortress, my God in whom I trust."

For he will deliver you from the snare of the fowler and from the deadly pestilence; he will cover you with his pinions, and under his wings you will find refuge; his faithfulness is a shield and a buckler. You will not fear the terror of the night nor the arrow that flies by day, nor the pestilence that stalks in darkness, nor the destruction that wastes at noon day.

A thousand may fall at your side, ten thousand at your right hand; but it will not come near you. You will only look with your eyes and see the recompense of the wicked.

Because you have made the Lord your refuge, the Most

High your habitation, no evil will befall you, no scourge shall come near your tent.

For he will give his angels charge of you, to guard you in all your ways. On their hands they will bear you up, lest you dash your foot against a stone. You will tread on the lion and the adder, the young lion and the serpent you will trample under foot.

Because he cleaves to me in love, I will deliver him; I will protect him, because he knows my name. When he calls to me, I will answer him: I will be with him in trouble, I will rescue and honor him. With long life I will satisfy him, and show him my salvation.

THE WISDOM OF THE EDGAR CAYCE READINGS

. . . in the secret chambers of one's own heart are stored that that makes for the real activities of that soul-consciousness, so [it] is the Holy of Holies where one meets with that they worship as their God. 262-30

A CYCLE OF PSALMS

In the cycle of psalms, we found the power point of wisdom in Psalm One, mystical oneness and our relationship to angels in Psalm 8, and the comforting assurance of where "shepherded" thoughts can take us. The power point in Psalm 24 was prosperity and the majestic potential of the high, holy hill within.

If the "secret place" where we are present with God is the "high/deep place" of the heart, implied by the word *Sinai*, these psalms are definitely pointing us toward the "high place." Now Psalm 91 gets added to the map, and brings us down and inward.

There is a saying, "If you don't stand for something, you'll fall for anything." What happens when we have to take a stand on principle and risk ridicule, rejection, or isolation? Where do you go when the spirit within you, the voice of your angel leads you into a direction counter to conventional wisdom or personal comfort? If it is a choice between pleasing others or satisfying the deeper self when faced with a challenge, what are you prepared to do?

"The joy of the Lord" is not only found in the ecstatic, uplifting experiences of celebration, inspiration, and transcendence but also in the strength to confront the most challenging and problematic issues of our existence, to go confidently through the fire, or walk peacefully among the lions. As long as we are in the body, we will be subject to trials and ordeals to which the flesh is heir.

The possibility of sickness, disease, betrayal, rejection, disappointment, and unrequited love surrounds us. Psychological stresses, emotional upsets, and physical ills can "waste us at noon day" or be a terror in the night.

But whenever they appear, the assurance here is that, even at this level, if we stop to think it through, if we slow down enough to make it "an experience of self" there is a Force that will walk with us through that experience and give us the "joy" of dominion over the fears, the fantasies, and "fight or flight" reactions that take away our strength and peace of mind.

The Cayce readings indicate that "what was begun in the earth must be met in the earth." If our deviation from spiritual laws was begun in the earth, it must be corrected there, too, and not in some other plane of existence. And it doesn't do us any good to put it off while we are here.

One of the most universal themes in dreams is that of being pursued, being chased, and hunted by a predator/pursuer. Try as we may in the dream, the pursuer cannot be eluded nor do we ever escape, until we awaken. Dreams of this type are reflections of problems we are refusing to deal with "head on" in our waking life. We cannot elude the pursuer, because the pursuer is a part of us—a part we fear, deny, or reject, and it chases us through the night because it wants us to "turn around" (the meaning of repent) and "face" it. Until we do, it will continue to haunt us—in our dreams, in our emotional discomfort, in our insecurity, and, in the extreme, through our paranoia and schizophrenia.

Psalm 91 brings us right into the experiences which we most fear and assures us that even in those trials, we will find the resources we need to insure a positive outcome. This psalm contains power points to counterbalance all the paralyzing fears and doubts that keep us "locked in" and separated from the richness of our Higher Self.

To find them, we must look within our hearts and find what truly motivates us—love or fear, trust and faith, or fears and doubt.

He shall give his angels charge over you . . . (Ps. 91:11)

THE WISDOM OF THE EDGAR CAYCE READINGS

. . . each soul *has* an individual guide—but the more often does such rise or develop by the choosing. As has been given, "There is set before thee life and death, good and evil—choose thou!" But it is just as true, "His angels have been given charge concerning thee." 443-3 Keep self [surrounded] by those influences that may be had in Him, and only as He would have thee be used; for, as He has given, "I will not *leave* thee comfortless" and "I will give my angels charge concerning thee" and "Will ye be my people, I will be your God." The face of the self's *own* angel is ever before the throne. Commune oft with Him. 1917-1 . . . let this mind be in you that was in Him, that the Father-God is ever present and has given His angels charge concerning thee rather than those [influences] that may be of thine own making. And His Spirit will bear witness with thy spirit whether ye be in that realm where the material, the mental or the spiritual application may be made of that *thou* experienceth in the mysteries of thine inner self. 585-2 For, to each entity, each soul, there is ever the ministering angel before the throne of grace, the throne of God. The ministering angel is the purposefulness, the spirit with which ye would do anything in relationship to others. 3357-2 But that there is the ability within self to contact as high a soul as is sought, by will, by desire, by the use of that attained for *this* soul, for *this* entity to reach into the cosmic or the universal sources for its supply, for its needs, for its desires. 443-4

Q. How may I overcome the fear I have of falling down the steps?

A. Know, as He has given, that He will give His angels charge concerning thee and will bear thee up. Let that faith, that trust, which has sustained thee in the present, keep thee from fear of any kind. Not that precautions are not to be taken, for that's what railings are built for! Hold to them, but don't trust them. Trust in the Lord who giveth man judgment and the abilities to those to prepare such! 5108-1

When Jesus was confronted by Satan in the wilderness, Satan quoted from Psalm 91 to tempt Him. He used the same verse which, in the readings above, Cayce quoted to a woman with multiple sclerosis, who was fearful of falling down the stairs. "Throw yourself down from the roof of the temple, Jesus—you can do it! Is it not written that God will give his angels charge of thee lest you dash your foot against a stone!" And Jesus replied, "Thou shall not tempt the Lord." It is curious that Satan chose this promise to undermine Jesus' connection to the Source. But, if *the ministering angel is the purposefulness, the spirit with which ye would do anything in relationship to others,* this chief of all bad angels symbolizes a potential motivation within Jesus.

Tradition tells us that Moses recited the Ninety-first Psalm as a way to ward off evil influences as he ascended Mount Sinai. For Jesus, something opposite occurred. The power of the Scripture was used against Him. Using Cayce's definition of the angel, Satan represents the shadow side of Jesus, the side He had to "face" in the wilderness. He had just begun His ministry, He knew through His earlier experiences and training in the temples and mystery schools of the ancient world that He was a powerful and charismatic leader, and He had a deep sense of personal mission and destiny.

Now as He stepped out into public life, He had to go within and challenge the "tempter" within Him—the potential for self-centered expression. For what purpose, what outcome was He going to use this energy? To manifest His spiritual ideal, or for gratification, ego inflation, and material gain? It took Him forty days to resolve the duality, and He emerged empowered and whole (Matthew 4:1-11).

According to one Edgar Cayce reading, Psalm 91 played a significant role at another major "transition" time in Jesus' ministry. At the Last Supper, when the meal was over, Jesus and His disciples left the upper room singing a sacred song. "And when they had sung an hymn, they went out into the mount of Olives." (Matthew 26: 30, Mark 14:26)

Jesus found in the Ninety-first Psalm the perfect prayer of attunement to face the crucial ordeal and "testing" that lay in front of Him. At the onset of his ministry, this psalm was used to try to provoke Him to misuse His power. At the end of His ministry, He used the psalm to center Himself.

For us, the Last Supper represents that period of preparation and communion before facing a momentous issue or any major transition where a choice has to be made. Every choice we make is an important one, because what we choose creates our destiny. The outcome of all our choices affects not only us, as individual souls, but has consequences that impact the whole. As we lift ourselves up, we lift up others. As we go down, many go with us.

At the Last Supper it was a "now or never, do or die—if I fail in this one, I've lost it all" kind of experience. When all the cards are on the table, when the stakes are highest, the fears are the greatest, and you know the whole outcome depends on you—where would you go to find the clarity of mind and emotional resolve that insures that you will make the decision of the heart and do everything that is required to master the situation?

Close your eyes and take a few deep breaths. Imagine a situation where you feel the calling of your deeper heart, and the people closest to you have no way to understand or relate to what you know you must do. Because they do not understand, there is no way for them to support you. In fact, some of their efforts actually serve to undermine your resolve and put you to the test.

Now look at the issues that come up for you? Can you picture a situation like that, or remember one that you experienced that is similar? Mentally go through the experience of meeting the obstacles, noting where your fears and insecurities are greatest, and then create a focus on activity that changes the relationships until you feel and see yourself acting out of your deepest heart's guidance.

As you meditate, consider the words of Psalm 91 and what they may have meant to Moses as he went into "the thick darkness where God was" or to Jesus as He prepared Himself for what He knew lay before Him. Before the glory of the resurrection, there would be the kiss of betrayal, the abandonment by friends, the rejection by His culture and social group, crushing judgments by politicians and religious leaders, and the potential of intense physical suffering, mental torment, and humiliation and ridicule. Yet, as the readings indicate, He joked at the Last Supper, smiled as He carried the cross, and comforted those who wept along the way.

Ten thousand shall fall at thy right hand . . . (Ps. 91:7)

THE WISDOM OF THE EDGAR CAYCE READINGS

Empty thy minds, *empty* thy hearts of all that thou hast held that is of a secular nature, if ye would know the *true* knowledge of thy God.

For as ye hold to those things, to those conditions, to those experiences, yea to those ideas that have formed concepts that ye should not do this, ye *should* do that, ye should make this, ye should lend that, these are but barriers if ye would know the true knowledge of *why*, of *how*, thy Brother, thy Lord, thy Master, came into the earth; and what He would have thee do with that which may be poured out to thee in thy seeking.

For as has been said of old, if the Lord be with *one* He shall put ten *thousand* to flight.

What, then, will *ye* . . . do? Ye *are* as lights unto many. What is *thy* choice? 262-96

THE PSALM OF ATTUNEMENT
WHEN FACING DIFFICULT TIMES

Can one put ten thousand to flight? In modern-day Mozambique, a small group of warriors, many as young as fourteen years old, has changed the course of one of Africa's most brutal bush wars. The warriors, bearing only spears, walk into battle fortified by a belief that bullets melt in front of them. Their supernatural powers are given to them through a ritual which was received by their charismatic leader in a vision. So empowering is the ritual and so complete is their faith in the vision of their leader that this small army of approximately three thousand men armed only with spears has achieved what Mozambique's Soviet-supplied sixty-thousand-man army was unable to do: turn the tide of a fifteen-year civil war against the guerrillas of the Mozambique Resistance Movement.*

The power of the Naprama—which means irresistible force—as the army is called, is fortified by a mixture of biblical accounts, by stories of the thirteenth-century Children's Crusades, and by their spirit mediums—people who are possessed by the spirits of important and powerful ancestors. According to the Naprama, the guerillas have so much respect for spirit mediums, that they believe the Naprama are protected from their weapons. When the Naprama's brigades come

---

*Reported in the *Detroit News*, Dec. 8, 1990.

marching, the guerrillas flee in panic.

History gives us many accounts of great warriors who spent their lives in the midst of battles, and yet never felt a wound. George Washington, often in the front lines, came out of battle with his jacket punctured with bullet holes yet he was never grazed by a bullet. The great Sioux warrior Crazy Horse drew enormous power from his visions and was never scarred by an enemy's weapon. Wyatt Earp, the legendary lawman of the Old West, was in the midst of many violent settings but was never wounded.

Is there something about the energy of a belief system, like that of Psalm 91, that made them immune to imminent harm?

How would you explain it in light of the promises of the Ninety-first Psalm?

On a more internal, everyday level, when we keep our mind focused on spirit, we are able to put "ten thousand" distractions to flight. Just one thought, rising from within the soul, can negate the power of ten thousand influences coming from without.

What attitude or state of mind is necessary to trust the power of love in all the circumstances of our lives? Or to do the right thing in the face of criticism, lack of support, outright hostility, indifference, and belittling.

Celebrate Your Purpose

Turn again to that as found in the 150th Psalm, and give praise that He, thy Lord, thy God, has entrusted to thee that way, that belief innate in thy purposes. 262-121

PSALM 150

Praise the Lord! Praise God in His sanctuary;
Praise Him for His mighty deeds;
Praise Him according to His exceeding greatness.

Praise Him with trumpet sound; praise Him with lute and
    harp!
Praise Him with timbrel and dance;
Praise Him with strings and pipe!

Praise Him with sounding cymbals;
Praise Him with loud clashing cymbals!

Let everything that breathes praise the Lord!
Praise the Lord!

PRAISE, PURPOSE, AND JOY

The Book of Psalms, with all its depths and resonance, runs out in a triumphant chorus of rejoicing in Psalm 150. Just as *Let There Be Light, the Divine Image,* and the *Power of Dominion* are seeds in Genesis 1 that find their full expression in the final chapters of The Revelation, the exuberant joy of this final psalm suggests the ultimate "delight" voiced in Psalm 1. It is the fullness of love and light, expressed in terms of rapturous celebration.

The psalm can also be understood as the apex of an experience in meditation. It is metaphoric of an inward realization of the fullness of God's presence, an experience so consummate that it sends its life-giving current through every cell and atom of the body—so that one's whole being, everything in the organism that breathes—the body, the mind, the cells, the senses, the nervous system—celebrates the discovery.

Truly is it said that the loudest praise of God is often heard in the silence of meditation.

Psalm 150 needs very little interpreting. It is not something to be understood so much as to be expressed and experienced. However, the reading quoted above gives us a basis for turning this psalm into a power point.

Do you have a purpose in life? Of course you do!

Have you discovered that purpose yet? Only you can say yes or no.

Has this book helped you? I truly hope so. Many prayers have shaped it.

Being rock solid certain of your purpose in life is, indeed, something to celebrate. With such a purpose, your life has a meaning and direction that can't be distorted or aborted. Some feel a sense of purpose almost from their first breath. Others discover it through loss and disappointment, some find it revealed through a long and challenging quest. However it comes into our consciousness, it was written on the soul first, waiting to be awakened by the will.

Fulfilling your purpose on every level can only be done in cooperation with a higher power. And you belong to a support group of all who serve that power.

MAKE IT AN EXPERIENCE:
PRAISE AND THANKSGIVING

In a group, appoint one person to be a leader and read each section individually, pausing a few moments to give everyone an opportunity to make a verbal response. (If you are alone, do the following quietly as a silent meditation.)

To begin, start with a short prayer and allow participants to focus inwardly. Perhaps the leader can do a relaxation or attunement induction, suggesting that people close their eyes, focus on their breathing, and relax.

Leader: *Praise God in His sanctuary.* Close your eyes, take a breath, and go within to that sanctuary where God is. Silently, to yourself, affirm that your body is the temple, the sanctuary of the Living God, and in that place called the Holy of Holies, God is. Go there now, and with your own words and your own way of expressing, known only to you, silently praise God in the sanctuary of your inner being.

(Allow an appropriate span of silent time.)

Leader: *Praise God in the firmament.* In this round, we will make "firm" our praise with the power of our voice. We will give "form" to our feelings. As we go around the circle, make "firm" your feelings of gratitude, thanksgiving, or praise through verbal expression or a physical movement or gesture. (If you are alone, speak it with feeling or sing words of praise from your personal experience.)

If you are sure of your purpose or mission in life, praise God for the confidence you have in your abilities.

(Members of the group take turns expressing.)

Leader: *Praise Him for His mighty deeds.* As we go around the circle this time, speak a word of blessing or praise for what the power of Love, the power of the Creative Spirit, the power of God has brought into your life. What is it of the Divine that you most stand in awe and wonder of?

Leader: *Praise Him according to His exceeding greatness.* Let us focus for a moment now on the realization that we are all made in the Image of God. And focus now how some part of that Image is being reflected by each person in this group. How great is God who made us all in His Image. Now as we take a turn going around the circle, let each one honor God's greatness by recognizing some aspect of the Divine in each person here. What part of God's Image shines most through them? What attribute or quality of the Divine shines most brightly through them—*for you!* When it is your turn, honor that presence by recognizing it with simple words of praise and appreciation.

When it is your turn to receive from the group, honor their sharing by simply accepting their truth and allowing it in. (If you are alone, mentally review the people in your life and give praise for "that of God" which you see in them.)

Leader: *Praise Him with trumpet sound; Praise Him with timbrel and dance;*

Praise Him with strings and pipe! Let us now make a joyful noise unto the Lord!

(It is everyone's choice what sounds to make. This can be planned ahead, and group members can bring various noise- and music-making instruments, or simply

262 / Spiritual Power Points

shout and sing, clap, cheer, dance. Hug, smile, exchange
with one another. Be as free and spontaneous as you can!
Enjoy it all!)

ALL: *Let everything that breathes praise the Lord!*
Praise the Lord!
Take a deep breath together, and all do a rolling OM
chant, or a cheer, or sing a favorite song.

A CULMINATING JOY: CELEBRATE YOUR PURPOSE

Take a moment and read the words of Psalm 150. What
are the mental pictures you have as you read it?
Now read it again, and focus on the feeling it expresses.
Now spend a few moments exploring each of the fol-
lowing suggestions:
Imagine a time when you felt totally joyful.
Imagine what it would be like to be as joyful as the
spirit of this psalm.
What is your purpose in life as you understand it now?
In what way was your purpose made known to you?
Are you absolutely certain that there are spiritual
forces as well as supportive people on this earth, who
have been, are, and will be drawn to you and willing to
help you because of the power and purpose your life has?
Does it seem logical and natural to agree that life has
meaning and value? How does knowing your purpose
add to it?
How deeply confident are you that you have the will
and the determination and the means to find and fulfill
your purpose in Life?

*(In a sharing session, once the above is completed, a
designated leader can then guide the rest in this visualization.)*

Now relax comfortably, close your eyes, and in your imagination see everyone who has ever loved you, everyone you have ever known or respected or admired, everyone who has been a role model for you—and imagine them all cheering you on.

Imagine characters from your past, people in the news, key figures and prominent people in the world today along with your favorite characters from the Bible, from literature, mythology, folklore and fairy tales, all gathered together in one joyful assembly to celebrate your purpose and to cheer you on.

Now put in your favorite band or musical group. Add several gospel choirs and a symphony. Now hear the drums, the brass, the woodwinds. Bring up the music, make it even louder. Bring the people in closer. Make the faces brighter, the smiles larger. Turn up the lights. See yourself in the center of this great celebration. Now imagine the person whom you could never imagine—the most incongruous person of all—as the main cheerleader and the conductor. See that person holding up a big sign with your purpose written on it for everyone to see—now everyone begins to chant

YOU CAN DO IT. YES, YOU CAN.

YOU CAN DO IT. YES, YOU CAN.

Now you repeat it and repeat it along with them, over and over again, until you are absolutely saturated, overflowing, and totally filled with a supernatural confidence and assurance that God, too, is cheering you on and the purpose you serve is One with His (Hers).

Continue until your joy is full.

About the Author

An author, ordained minister, and spiritual counselor, Robert Krajenke has been appreciated by audiences throughout the United States and Europe for his wisdom, inspiration, warmth, and humor. A man of many insights, Robert is the author of *Edgar Cayce's Story of the Old Testament,* a three-volume study based on the clairvoyant discourses of the renowned American mystic, Edgar Cayce.

Robert has counseled individuals and conducted workshops and seminars in many parts of the United States and Europe and has guided tours to sacred sites in Israel, Egypt, and France. His areas of special interest include many facets of the holistic paradigm, including myth, dreams, meditation, spiritual healing, relationship dynamics, vibrational healing, and the development of experiential approaches to enhanced spiritual awareness, creativity, and emotional health.

A native of Michigan, Robert lives in Detroit with his wife, Lynne, an Integrative Vibrational Therapist.

If you've enjoyed this book or if you have comments, suggestions, or ideas to share concerning your experience with *Spiritual Power Points,* or if you desire information on Robert's speaking schedule, or his availability as a speaker for your church, group, or organization, please contact him through the A.R.E.

Books of Related Interest

Edgar Cayce's Story of the Old Testament, a series by Robert W. Krajenke. This series of books traces the Old Testament from the beginning of creation to the birth of Jesus, showing the Bible as a pattern for the mind's unfoldment and a portrayal of the soul's journey.

From the Birth of Souls to the Death of Moses
Identifies a powerful plan at work throughout history, set in motion to restore humankind's fallen consciousness to its true state.

ISBN 0-87604-114-4   Paperback   Order #293 $8.95

From Joshua to the Golden Age of Solomon
Insights from the Cayce readings into symbolism found in the books of Judges, Ruth, and Samuel. Reveals Hannah's modern-day incarnation.

ISBN 0-87604-115-2   Paperback   Order #294 $8.95

From Solomon's Glories to the Birth of Jesus
The beginnings of the Essene community, the wanderings of the lost tribes, death of Solomon, and the rise of the prophets.

ISBN 0-87604-116-0   Paperback   Order #295 $9.95

To order any of these books or to receive a free catalog, call us at

1-800-723-1112

Or write

A.R.E. Press
Sixty-Eighth & Atlantic Avenue
P.O. Box 656
Virginia Beach, VA 23451-0656

(All prices subject to change)